PRIESTS—WHAT LIES AHEAD?

PRIESTS— WHAT LIES AHEAD?

A Dialogue of Carlos Granados with Luis F. Ladaria, George Pell, Livio Melina, and Charles J. Chaput

Translated by Richard Goodyear

IGNATIUS PRESS   SAN FRANCISCO

Original Spanish edition:
Sacerdotes, ¿con qué futuro?
© 2016 Biblioteca de Autores Cristianos, Madrid

Cover photograph by Stefano Spaziani

Cover design by Enrique J. Aguilar

CONTENTS

PREFACE

I would like, in these few words, simply to describe how this book came to be. It originated in an intuition that, in the changes that our society and the Church are undergoing, we can discern the potential for a new fruitfulness for the priest. And he will be able to realize that potential if he roots himself in what he is: teacher, father, physician, and pastor. These are four images of the Only Priest, of Christ the Lord, who is the true Teacher, Father, Physician, and Pastor.

In order to examine those images closely, I have chosen four priests, great exemplars, who speak with the authority of their experience and of the impressive fruitfulness of their lives. The literary genre of a conversation or interview is always an occasion for lively and dynamic elaboration: it enables us to give voice to concerns and questions that might be out of place in a magisterial exposition. But it was also a matter of offering in this way a more lively and direct witness, in familiar language, to pose questions about hope to these especially prominent priests. They explain to us in this book what makes the priest's life great and beautiful, as teacher, father, physician, and pastor.

The priest is a teacher. To understand this very important aspect of the life of an ordained minister, I turned to Archbishop Luis Ladaria, S.J., whom I had the good fortune to interview where he works, at the very seat of the Congregation for the Doctrine of the Faith in Rome. As a true teacher, Archbishop Luis Ladaria is calm and hard-working. In an extremely cordial tone—which is habitual in him—the interview proceeded briskly, without digressing or wasting time.

Pope Benedict XVI named him Secretary of the Congregation for the Doctrine of the Faith, with the rank of archbishop, on July 9, 2008. He had worked for years in the Congregation as a consultor and also as a member of the International Theological Commission. But above all he had spent his whole life teaching, in Madrid at Comillas Pontifical University or, in the last few decades, in Rome at the Pontifical Gregorian University. Father Ladaria has the soul of a professor. He is known at the Gregorian University for the high academic level and great clarity of his lectures, which he gave as someone who knows he is truly the "parish priest of his students". He is, therefore, as the reader will see, the right person to illuminate for us the fruitfulness of the priest as teacher.

The priest is a father: he propagates through the sacraments. The dialogue with Cardinal Pell addresses precisely this dimension. George Pell is the Cardinal Prefect of the Vatican Secretariat for the Economy, and he was for many years metropolitan archbishop of Melbourne and Sydney. His ordination as a priest was fifty years ago now, and he has lost none of his passion as a father.

I had the good fortune to interview him in Rome, in his personal residence. It was a day full of questions and with answers in English. Cardinal Pell's conversation is calm and unhurried, but with a fine economy of expression. His library is that of a scholar, educated in Rome and at Oxford. He has the demeanor of a pastor who is concerned about the specific real-world problems of the Church. He has the mind of a practical person; it is fitting that the economic affairs of the Holy See are his area of responsibility. And he has the heart of a father, focused on opening up the future.

The time flew by. His answers were very pleasing. The cardinal had prepared for the questions and even delivered to the interviewer a "supplementary bibliography" to bridge any gaps that he might have left. Yes, Cardinal Pell has lived a true fatherhood as a priest in these fifty years of ministry: his selection for this book could not have been better.

The priest is also a physician: he heals wounds, he cures, like the Good Samaritan, and he brings his neighbor back to the inn that is the Church. To help us understand this aspect of priestly life, few priests can speak to us with as much knowledge and experience as Monsignor Livio Melina. Professor Melina holds the Chair in Moral Theology at the Pontifical John Paul II Institute for Studies on Marriage and Family, and at the time of the interview was its president. He is more than just erudite, in the highest sense of the word: he is also outstanding in his knowledge of the human heart, thanks to his ample experience as a pastor and confessor. He has taught generations of priests and was one of the founders of a broad pastoral movement in support of families.

I was fortunate enough to interview him at the seat of the Pontifical John Paul II Institute in Rome, in the Lateran. There I was able to speak with him for an entire day, at a pace that was nothing if not intense. If there is anything surprising about Don Livio Melina—and in this he very much reminds one of the pope emeritus, Benedict XVI—it is his ability to fashion a statement that is seamlessly woven together, transparent, intelligent, original, full of hope. Our interview reveals the heart of a physician, of one who shares in the Passion of Christ, of the "wounded surgeon", who heals us precisely through his own wounds, in the image of the Anglo American poet T. S. Eliot.[1]

Finally, the priest is a pastor. To cover this aspect of the figure of a priest, I decided to fly to Philadelphia to talk with Archbishop Charles J. Chaput of that American diocese. The expectations I had formed from what I had heard about his virtues and gifts were not disappointed. The reader will be able to judge for himself. Archbishop Chaput was born into a Native American family. His grandmother lived on a reservation, and he became a member of the tribe as well. He was at first a Capuchin friar, entering holy orders; he later was named bishop of Rapid City, then of Denver, and now of Philadelphia. Archbishop Chaput is a fine priest, with all the experience of life and wisdom acquired over many years. He is a pastor from head to toe, with the proverbial prudence of a wise tribal chief, a deep knowledge of the human heart, and wide-ranging interests.

He received me in the diocesan seminary, where he himself lives. We had our discussion there, in peace and quiet. His manner is direct, clear, concise. His eyes shine in a particular way, even sparkling with singular life at certain points in the conversation. Leaning back informally in an armchair, he not only invites confidence; he almost invites confidences. Archbishop Chaput is a direct, accessible man of great humanity and a profound sense of the divine. He thus has shown himself to be a matchless priest for talking with us about this pastoral aspect of the ministry.

---

[1] The wounded surgeon plies the steel
   That questions the distempered part;
   Beneath the bleeding hands we feel
   The sharp compassion of the healer's art.

   The Four Quartets: "East Coker IV"

This completes the description of some aspects of the shape and genesis of the book. All that remains (last but not least) is to mention the warm and gracious foreword by Cardinal Müller, Prefect of the Congregation for the Doctrine of the Faith, who has been kind enough to lend words of his own to this book. They are also the words of an experienced priest, of a teacher and father, of a true physician and seasoned pastor. They make a magnificent portal to the reflections of his brothers in the priesthood. The interviews gathered here, preceded by the cardinal's foreword, have been arranged in the chronological order in which they were conducted, as was dictated by various surrounding circumstances.

Finally, I also wholeheartedly thank all those who have joined together in this book, with their advice, their words, and their encouragement, to bring it to completion. The future of the priest, and his fruitfulness, is a question for all of us: my aspiration has been that a reading of this book will shine a light on the paths to the fruitfulness that the Spirit is capable of generating in the lives of today's priests.

CARLOS GRANADOS
December 8, 2016
Feast of the Immaculate Conception

FOREWORD

"I became your father in Christ Jesus through the gospel" (1 Cor 4:15). These words of Saint Paul testify to a great fruitfulness—the fruitfulness of the priest—that has never stopped yielding fruit in the life of the Church and of the world. They are words of hope, because they assure the continual presence of the great gift that Jesus left us in the Last Supper: "... and the bread which I shall give for the life of the world is my flesh" (Jn 6:51). From generation to generation, innumerable priests have transmitted this abundant life, making it their own, and in doing so have enabled the world to continue to await God's great gifts. The priest, in his representation of Christ's fatherhood and acting *in persona Christi capitis* (*Presbyterorum ordinis* 2), is the man of the future.

In the presence of this uninterrupted chain of fatherhood, we may wonder, what future can the priest foster in the Church of our time? Can he continue to be a fount of hope for men? There are numerous voices today that call for the sterilization of this priestly presence and mission. The dominant culture asks the priest to reduce the abundance of life that he brings and limit himself to ameliorating man's life on earth, without opening him to the great hope that Jesus brought. They ask him to refrain from touching on this vital point of a person's identity, where he opens himself to the greatness of life and God's presence and action in it. They urge the priest to assume a false humility that leads him to be skeptical of the magnitude

of the gift he has received. The priest is accepted by this
dominant culture to the extent that he performs a social
function, accompanying the sick or managing the parish's
charitable activity. But he is precisely not accepted as a
priest—that is, as a minister consecrated by God to engender the life of Christ in men and society.

Notwithstanding, without the priesthood, hope would
disappear from the Church, because what would also disappear is the Word and voice of Jesus, who leaves us his
flesh for the life of the world. Without the priesthood, our
little hopes would not be revivified by the great hope sown
by Christ. The priest, as Thomas Aquinas has taught us, is
the man of the common good of the Church, who has
been entrusted with proposing and cultivating, in every
person and in all of ecclesial life, the greatness of the life in
communion that God has given us.

In this book, four very experienced priests undertake
to shed light on the hope that the priest can bring to the
Church and to the world. They make it clear to us that
the question of the identity of the priest, which became
so intense after Vatican II, cannot be resolved through an
introspection that would revolve around the narcissistic
question: "Who am I?" The four priests who speak in
these pages ask us to take another perspective. The priest,
as a father who generates the future, only knows who he
is when he is capable of that generation. His question is
not, "Who am I?" but, "How can I make this great gift
I have been granted ripen and bear the most fruit?" That
is what Pope Francis also reminded us of in the Mass he
celebrated to mark the retirement of several priests on
the day of the Sacred Heart of Jesus: "The epicenter
of the priest's heart is outside of himself: he is not drawn
by his own 'I', but by the 'Thou' of God and by the 'we'
of other men and women."

And that is what brings to the fore the questions that these pages address regarding the future of the priest as generator of a future for the world. Why is the priest a father, and what kind of life, corporeal and spiritual, can he communicate to man and to culture? How can he, as a teacher, radiate light that will open up broad horizons and long paths? How can he generate communion, as a pastor, so that the love that makes life great and beautiful will blossom? How can he regenerate hope, like a physician, in the man who lives hemmed in, prisoner of an instant that repeats itself again and again, without a future?

What is at stake here, certainly, is the future of every priest. And in the future of every priest, in turn, the future of the Church and of society is at stake. It is not a small question, and the answer we will find in this book measures up to it. We thank Biblioteca de Autores Cristianos for bringing us these voices full of hope. May God will that the consecration that we were once granted be renewed in us, we who have received the grace of ordained ministry. And may we live it in the fullest faithfulness.

GERHARD CARDINAL MÜLLER
Prefect of the Congregation
for the Doctrine of the Faith

I

THE PRIEST AS TEACHER •
OF A DOCTRINE OF LIFE

A Conversation with
Archbishop Luis F. Ladaria, S.J.,
Secretary of the Congregation for the
Doctrine of the Faith

1. A singular parish

Who are the priests who have had the greatest influence on your
life as a priest? I mean not only at the moment of your vocation,
but also priests who have left their mark on your way of being a
priest because they opened up a horizon to you, stood behind you
in your moments of difficulty and struggle, or taught you the art
of being a priest. Why did those priests have such an influence
on you?

A great many people have had an influence on my vocation and my life as a priest. Rather than a single great figure who has had a decisive influence on my reply to God,
there have been a host of them, a large number of priests
whom I have had the providential good fortune to know.
There are the Jesuit Fathers who taught me in school, parish priests, those who have accompanied me later on in my

life as a religious and as a priest. I cannot specifically name some without omitting many others. And that in itself is a remarkable fact: what has most shaped my vocation has been an environment, a human circle, a living communion, a fabric woven of people. We are drawn not only to individuals, but also to the way they work together in the same vineyard, and this is part of the calling to the priesthood, a calling to the shared mission, to friendship in the Lord, and more.

But there certainly have been priests with whom I have identified more than with others. For example, I feel a particular debt of gratitude to Father Antonio Orbe, S.J., the director of my thesis. Father Orbe imparted to me a vision of Christianity that begins with its culmination, with Christ resurrected, the perfect man, and from there lights the path of man in its entirety, as it is slowly given expression in God's hands. The priest is called to collaborate in this work of God as a goldsmith, channeling everything toward its end in Jesus, who ceaselessly draws us to himself.

And the popes? You have lived with six popes. Has there been one who has had a particular impact on your priestly life?

All of them have, but perhaps pride of place falls to Paul VI because he was the pope with whom I grew up, first when I was young and later as a priest. He is the pope in whose time I received my education, began my years of teaching, and matured, and all of that left a singular imprint, the imprint of our beginnings that stays with us always. Later there were others, of course. And I am deeply devoted to all of them, but the figure of Paul VI always stands out for having been decisive at such an important moment of my life, when my vocation and thinking were forged.

You have lived your priesthood primarily as a teacher. I once heard that you saw your classroom as a parish and your students as your congregation. It is a beautiful image: I would like to ask you about the fruitfulness of teaching. Have you been able to live your priestly fatherhood in it, too? And how have you lived it when you were researching and studying theology? Where have you most experienced that a priest is always a father?

I have made this comparison many times myself, and I say that because I have sometimes been asked whether classroom teaching has not prompted in me a certain nostalgia for the pastoral life, as though I must have been missing pastoral work. I have always said that I have not missed devoting myself more specifically to pastoral work, because I honestly believed that the students before me in the classroom were like my parishioners. I have obviously enjoyed being able to hear confession and to devote myself, for example, more directly to sacramental practice. But my class has for me been pastoral work, an apostolate. That approach to teaching is how I have lived, so I have used the comparison you mention many times. I think the work of a priest covers a very broad range, and it especially involves introducing people into God's mystery, helping to acquaint them with the Word of God in all its richness. Bearing in mind also that there were many priests, seminarians, and religious among my listeners, I clearly was living my work in teaching as a priestly ministry, as a form of pastoral charity. The ministry of a priest is a ministry of light, for it illuminates the ultimate end point of all the paths of men.

I should add that, yes, the pastoral and the academic can be distinguished from one another, but only up to a certain point, because anyone living a priestly life is living a pastoral life in everything, living always as a father. In that sense, when I think of the hundreds of people I have accompanied in earning their degrees and writing their doctoral theses, it is borne in upon me that I have lived a true spiritual fatherhood, the fruitfulness of which reached as far as those with whom my students engaged later on. Saint Paul long ago joined spiritual fatherhood with preaching and with the teaching of God's Word, which is like a seed that the priest sows in those who hear him. I have seen students passing through classrooms and libraries for decades, each of them with his worries and outlook. And in my work in the classroom, and in guiding them in their doctoral theses, I saw how there was fostered in them a clearer vision of the greatness of the mystery of God and, at the same time, a greater experience of that mystery. I saw a new maturity being born in my students, the maturity of wise men, capable of bringing light to others. Yes, here, too, there is a fatherhood of light, there is pastoral work. The priest is father as well as pastor, and I have of course lived my teaching career that way, as father and as pastor.

2. How does the gospel yield fruit?

Christ the Teacher: What does that evoke in you? Have you heard his doctrine as something external, foreign to what you truly wanted? Is he just another teacher, or is he "the" Teacher, the only true Teacher?

That is right, Christ is not just "a" teacher, not just one more teacher; Christ is "the" Teacher. We have to see Christ that way, acknowledge him as the Lord, as the only Lord. The Gospels contain two key homilies that in a way define the teachings of Christ: the Sermon on the Mount and his farewell discourse at the Last Supper. They are the core of his preaching. On both occasions, Jesus insists that he is the Teacher and the Lord, that he is the way, that he can speak with the same authority as God ("you have heard ... [b]ut I say to you" [Mt 5:33–34]). We have to make it clear, however, that these very important words of Jesus can only be understood when they are considered in the light of his "acts", of the life of the Lord, his miracles, his gestures, his gaze, and above all the Passion and the Resurrection. It is words and deeds together that make him "the" Teacher.

I usually started my classes with a reference to the New Testament, which rooted what I was going to say in each lecture. It was a reference to a verse related to what we were going to study in that class. I think that everything, therefore, was also centered on a reference to the true Teacher, who is the one who speaks to us in the words of Holy Scripture, the singular words of the New Testament. I think that, as a result of this simple reference at the outset, the class was attuned from the beginning to the Word of Jesus, the only Teacher. Saint Augustine said that every teacher places himself at the service of the true Teacher, who is the Holy Spirit, who speaks to a person's heart. As priests, we know that our teaching is a ministry, so that, in the Spirit, Jesus' voice may resonate within every person.

Archbishop Ladaria, after your many years in close proximity to the Church Fathers—to Hilary, Irenaeus, Justin, Augustine— why is it important for a priest to read assiduously and be familiar with the writings of the Church Fathers? What can we learn about the priesthood from the very lives of these great pastors, who were also theologians?

The Church Fathers are centrally important. We priests are told this by the Church indirectly, but very clearly, by the provision of readings from the Church Fathers in the Divine Office, in the daily liturgy for priests. It is true that patristic readings are not always called for, but they are in the great majority of cases. There must be a reason for that practice on the part of the Church. In addition, the Church calls them "Fathers"; they are the "Church Fathers". This, too, is significant because it attributes the paternity of the Church to them. The fact that the Church does so and calls on us in that fashion, treating such references as indispensable, means all the more that we must do the same. Besides, let us bear in mind that in the time of the Church Fathers, the great dogmatic questions were answered in the great councils. There the Church shaped her faith, the Symbol, the *regula fidei*. That, too, is very important. In addition to these great issues, the Church Fathers offer us magnificent pages on the subject of priestly ministry, on the spirituality and life of the priest. We find, especially in the writings of Saint Augustine, perceptive texts on the subject of how to orient and live our priesthood. The priest, who is a father, is called to keep constantly in mind this foundational form of paternity in Christianity that the Church Fathers present to us. Only through them can we also be fathers of the communities entrusted to us. In general, we can recognize in the Church Fathers true teachers for our priestly life.

Moreover, we should also bear in mind that there is in the Church Fathers a true theology of the priesthood, especially since the time of Ignatius of Antioch, which saw the emergence of clear distinctions among the offices of bishop, priest, and deacon. The patristic period sees the development of an entire priestly doctrine and spirituality, a way of living the priestly mission. For Saint Augustine and Saint Hilary, for example, to cite two of the Church

Fathers whom you mentioned, the unity of doctrine and life was fundamental: without doctrine, the priest could not accomplish his mission as a teacher; and without a life lived in accordance with the faith, teaching would be rendered useless. Upright doctrine and upright life were two keys to a sound definition of the priest.

According to what you have said, the Church Fathers teach us to live our priestly fatherhood. Could you develop a bit more what it is that they teach us, what they see as the key elements of priestly life?

I would mention first the fact that we often see in the Church Fathers the integration of the pastor and the theologian. These two gifts or ministries were frequently found together in them: the closeness of the pastor and the profundity of the theologian are mingled in their writings. We have today, too, some great figures of whom the same is true. The case of Joseph Ratzinger comes to mind, for example, who as a bishop continued to write invaluable books of theology and who, even as pope, bestowed texts of unparalleled depth and beauty on us. In the same way, the Church Fathers, too, were pastors and at the same time theologians. And a beneficial circle was established between those two facets. Saint Augustine, for example, would never have developed into the theologian he was if he had not been a pastor. Being a pastor helped him be a theologian, and vice versa. This, too, is an important lesson for us. Every priest who is a pastor is also called to be a theologian—that is, a person who speaks of God or, rather, who speaks God's Word because he hears him and transmits his message to his fellow men.

I think reference to Joseph Ratzinger's work can help us here, as well, because it is a subject on which he has

reflected in particular. Joseph Ratzinger wrote an important article in 1968 on the significance of the Fathers for
theology today. He was concerned then about the tendencies that seemed to be in the Church to see the New
Testament as sufficient and to lack a sense of the two
thousand years that followed. Ratzinger always found this
tendency to be a temptation because it led to the bimille-
nary tradition of the history of the Church being blithely
thrown overboard. Actually, if we believe that the Church
has been guided by the Spirit throughout her temporal
history, we cannot say that tradition can be discarded, that
it has moved away from its origin, for the contrary is true.
We must recover all that tradition. We cannot be indif-
ferent to the Church Fathers, because they constitute the
foundation of our response to God's revelation and make
that response possible. In addition, they hold the seed of
a great many intuitions that are still to be developed, and
returning to them turns out to be very fruitful.

In my case, for example, in studying the works of Hilary of Poitiers and his struggle against Arianism, I was
able to see the strength of the Trinitarian affirmation and
Saint Hilary's defense of Jesus' eminence. In reading Hilary, I have learned how to practice theology. For me,
one of the most enlightening aspects of studying his theology was to see that, for him, the most important thing
was not directly the divinity of the Son but, rather, the
paternity of the Father. The divinity of the Son obviously
derived from the paternity of the Father. But it was the
latter's paternity that was, for Hilary, the central point.
And this was a true discovery for me, one of the insights
that opened the way forward for me in studying theology. There was in it a seed that has proved very fruitful
for me in all aspects of my life as a priest, not just in
deepening my theology. I would like to recall, for example, this sentence from Hilary: The Son consummates the

Father (*Patrem consummat Filius*). Is it not true that, in our priestly experience, too, we experience the enrichment of our fatherhood through what we give, what we cause to grow in our children?

Recalling Socrates' image, a priest who is a teacher is like one who gives birth to a new being, who gives birth to truth in a man's heart, but what life does he father? Because there is a way of life that is "not human", there are ways of life that are not in accordance with the gospel. What does it mean to foster someone in a holy life by means of the Word? Or what does it mean, as Saint Paul says, to engender through the gospel [see 1 Cor 4:15]?

Engendering supernatural life through the sacraments is the fundamental work of the priest; he engenders children into divine life. The priest's ministry is usually structured along the lines of his three functions, which are to "sanctify" (in the sacraments), to "teach" (by word and deed), and to "govern"—that is, to orient and guide individuals on the Christian path. With that, priests truly nourish God's people. Priestly service (*diakonia*) is rendered in these priestly *tria munera*.

Now, you have emphasized in your question that a priest's fatherhood is also realized because he teaches a truly human way of life. This seems clear to me and important: the priest teaches a human way of life by teaching a Christian way of life. If Jesus Christ is the "perfect man", then teaching how to live like Christ can only be an illumination of the way to live a fully human life. In *Gaudium et spes*, the Second Vatican Council affirms in a truly illuminating statement: "Whoever follows after Christ, the perfect man, becomes himself more of a man" (no. 41). And the same pastoral constitution says, in number 22: "The truth is that only in the mystery

of the incarnate Word does the mystery of man take on
light. For Adam, the first man, was a figure of Him Who
was to come, namely, Christ the Lord. Christ, the final
Adam, by the revelation of the mystery of the Father and
His love, fully reveals man to man himself and makes his
supreme calling clear."

It is Christ who gives us, through the Word, through
the sacrament, the key to what is human. We can say that
Jesus, on the one hand, gives us the fullness of what we
seek and desire. On the other hand, it is also true that Jesus
came to purge us, through conversion, of everything that
distances us from our vocation. This requires man, for his
part, to undergo a purification and take a certain path. And
it requires the priest, for his, to prepare the path to the true
Teacher by way of sacrament and Word. Finally, Jesus not
only consummates human aspirations; he surpasses them,
goes beyond our desires, because the fullness of man is
communion with God, is something that lies beyond man's
strength. And the priest, too, participates in all these works
of Christ. The priest is an expert in humanity because he
is an expert in Jesus, and his mission is to consummate all
that is human, purify it, and lead it to the divine. It is truly
a great mission, which is accomplished through preaching and the sacraments. And, it is important to remember,
through prayer as well, through the priest's life of prayer
and the way he himself lives the Eucharist. We read in the
Liturgy of the Hours: "This is he who loves his brothers:
he who prays often for his people." These are words that
particularly apply to priests.

3. What is the glory of God?

*Sometimes our congregations tell us we preach a doctrine that is
disconnected from life, that we speak to them about a distant God*

who has nothing to do with their daily life, and that we propose an excessively ideal life to them, as a goal to be reached, but that is still far away and almost beyond their strength to attain. This certainly fosters weariness and disillusionment in them. How can what we preach be connected to the path of life? How do we foster awareness that what we preach is not just an abstract ideal but, rather, the foundation *on which our life is built?*

Pope Francis has emphasized to us that the shepherd must be with his sheep, that he must be aware of the problems in their lives, of the difficulties through which they are going. That is the only way doctrine is made flesh and becomes personal. That makes it clear that we are preaching, not an ideal, but an incarnate doctrine, which also seeks the lost sheep, which draws near to everything and everyone because it knows that we are all called to the full life Jesus has brought us.

It is important here to emphasize one aspect of this: the Christian "ideal", so to speak, is not unattainable. It is unattainable, certainly, with our strength alone. That would be a Pelagian ideal, the ideal of one who thinks he can be self-sufficient. But if there is anything about which we priests must preach, if we must insist on anything, it is the truth that grace exists, the grace of Jesus Christ. And we must insist that with that grace we can do good and be good, we can live up to the gospel, we can live in accordance with the Word of the Lord, according to his commandments. This is a point we have sometimes neglected. In that sense, I insist: holiness is an ideal that is attainable through grace, through the strength that God gives us. The view that faith is an ideal inaccessible to man is a Protestant view. For us Catholics, however, Christianity is a realizable ideal, made flesh. There are three different meanings of the word "ideal": the Pelagian meaning, in which the ideal is pursued with one's own strength; the

Protestant meaning, which sees the ideal as being unrealizable because man will always remain a sinner; and the Catholic meaning, in which the ideal is incarnate in a person's life because God's grace has transformed him and accompanies him always.

Actually, we are saying precisely that when we venerate the saints: there it is; there is the life of one who was capable of living the reality of the gospel, in all its exigency and radicalism. And a vocation for holiness is not just for a few. This certainly does not mean that misery and limits and weakness do not exist. Among human beings, only the Virgin Mary was born and lived without sin, while the rest of us fall down and pick ourselves up again. But with God's grace, we realize an ideal that is attainable, that is not some faraway thing, abstract and beyond our capacity to attain.

It is therefore important that in catechism and our pastoral work we insist on God's grace, on the gift of God that makes it possible to live up to his call. And it is good to illustrate this reality by reference to the saints, in accordance with what the great Catholic catechetical tradition has done. If we look solely to man's fragility and what he himself is capable of giving of himself, we will not be able to raise our hopes or escape the logic of an "unattainable ideal". It is therefore necessary to preach and live the grace of God that makes man's life great.

What if the priest were to be afraid to preach the whole truth to his congregation? There are times when there is an evident contrast between the way parishioners think and live, on the one hand, and what Christ preaches, on the other. What happens if the priest accommodates himself to general opinion? Actually, what man wants most coincides with what Jesus proclaims and with the greatness of truth. What does it mean to "raise up" man, to open up to him a new space in which his life can be greater? How can preaching make that possible?

Fear of preaching the truth can come to all of us, because it is always there. In the Second Letter to Timothy (2 Tim 4:2), Saint Paul exhorts us to preach in season and out of season. Society will often tell the priest that he is preaching out of season, out of place, out of context. He will then need to turn to the *parrhesia* that Pope Francis mentions to us so often, the prophetic courage, the spiritual freedom to denounce and speak truthfully, to call a spade a spade, even if it goes against the current of relativism that rules in our day.

Let us keep in mind that what man desires most is what Jesus gives us. The first experience of a convert is that what he has discovered is what he was yearning for. And that is what the priest is called to communicate: to impart something that raises man up, that makes it possible for him to attain what he most desires. There is no doubt that we have the best message, the good news, the best news for man.

We have perhaps gone through a period in which our preaching was too focused on the realities of sin, an overly "hamartiocentric" period. Now, certainly, a more positive impetus has asserted itself, a vision of the great life that Christ opens up to us. There is obviously a danger that we will go somewhat to the opposite extreme, forgetting the need for purification and conversion in Christian life. But in any case, we need to emphasize the positive vision, the fact that every person should be brought as close to Christ as possible and, therefore, to the fullest humanity. It was Saint Irenaeus of Lyon who illuminated this relationship most clear-sightedly in a phrase that has become celebrated: "Gloria Dei, vivens homo": The glory of God is a living man. That is, the more there is of God, the more humanity; the closer man is to God, the more he is fulfilled and realizes his true humanity. This can be seen very clearly if we read on in Irenaeus, who adds: "vita hominis, visio Dei": The life of man consists of seeing God.

You have written a good deal on the relationship between Christ and man. Is this formulation— "Preach Christ so as to edify men"—a valid one? Does preaching Christ build the human being? What value does this have for priests' preaching? Basically, to make the question a little more penetrating, if you will: Can we say that Christian preaching is not just one way of being a man but is, rather, the only way to be truly a man?

Certainly, the first reason for our preaching of Jesus is to make Christ known, loved, followed, and so on. But actually, when we do this, as Saint Paul said, we are building Christ, Christ who is the head of his whole Body, which is the Church. And so we could indeed say that we are therefore also building man, because Christ is the measure of man. In building what Saint Augustine called the whole Christ, we build the fullness of all that is human. It thus is clear that we begin, not with man, but rather with Jesus. It is not that from man we go on to discover Christ, but rather that from Christ we go on to discover man. We are called to union with Christ, and he therefore reveals to us who we are in the deepest depths of our being. Perhaps a more complete elaboration of it would be: "To preach Christ in order to build Christ in man", because the core is the preaching of Christ and the growth of Christ in man.

On the other hand, with respect to your other question, it is true that the fullness of all that is human is in Christ. Jesus is the only possible way for us to be fully human, to realize our most primal vocation. It will be said that there are persons in whom, even though they do not know Christ, we can clearly see some rays of humanity. That is true. But, as the Church Fathers said, those rays are the fruit of the seeds of the Word, sown by God to be ripened in Christ. The ultimate goal, fullness, the definitive end point of all that is human, resides in the risen Christ.

Finally, I would like to say something about the fundamental question—that is, about the great subject you raise and that actually can be traced back to the affirmation that Jesus Christ is the only Savior, the only Name that leads us back to the fullness of man. That reality is expounded in very clear terms in the important document of the Congregation for the Doctrine of the Faith entitled *Dominus Iesus*, which speaks to the uniqueness and saving universality of Jesus Christ and the Church. That document gathers together important affirmations regarding this question, which are still current as a way of dealing with the subject that has emerged here. *Dominus Iesus* (no. 6) explains, for example, that

the theory of the limited, incomplete, or imperfect character of the revelation of Jesus Christ, which would be complementary to that found in other religions, is contrary to the Church's faith. Such a position would claim to be based on the notion that the truth about God cannot be grasped and manifested in its globality and completeness by any historical religion, neither by Christianity nor by Jesus Christ. Such a position is in radical contradiction with the foregoing statements of Catholic faith, according to which the full and complete revelation of the salvific mystery of God is given in Jesus Christ.

Christian revelation is the communication of this truth, so that even those who do not know Jesus can only be saved because Christ acts in them. This is precisely the problem. All of this is said without losing esteem for others or for other religions; on the contrary, it is precisely this love toward all and the desire for "all men to be saved and to come to the knowledge of the truth" (no. 13) that animate the mission and the desire for Christ to be known and loved.

If the priest preaches sound doctrine, what he preaches will be infused with the Spirit. This is not a matter of encouraging believers to take on a burden. What we proclaim is a "pneumatic doctrine", driven by the strength of the Spirit. The Church Fathers—thinking here of Saint Irenaeus of Lyon or Saint Hilary of Poitiers—knew full well the importance of the Spirit in the life and preaching of Jesus and, therefore, of the Christian. How can the preaching of the priest be opened to the action of the Spirit? In what way does the word of a poor priest transmit the Spirit?

This reference to the Holy Spirit is important. In the early Christian tradition, the name of "Christ" became the proper name of Jesus; we have come to call him "Jesus Christ". But we must not forget that this proper name originally was the word "anointed", which is the meaning of the Greek word Χρῆστος, "Christos". Christ is he who has been anointed by the Holy Spirit.

This matter of anointing is crucial to an understanding of the life and work of Jesus. Among the theologians and Church Fathers at the dawn of Christianity, it was often thought that it was dangerous to insist too much on the anointing. There were evident risks of "adoptionism", of falling into the error of denying Jesus' divinity and considering him as something like a son adopted at the moment of his baptism in the Jordan, when the Spirit descended on him. This blurred the moment of anointing, at times confusing it with the Incarnation. And it gave rise to the question: What sense did it make for Jesus to have received the Spirit at the age of thirty? Today we have recovered the importance of many passages in the Gospels that speak in terms of the presence and action of the Spirit in Christ's life. And, too, we have learned to increase our esteem for the ancient tradition of the Church Fathers, who spoke in terms of an anointing of the flesh of the Word through the action of the Spirit in the Jordan, without falling at all into adoptionism—that is, clearly affirming that Jesus is God made man and that in his humanity he was united with the Spirit.

Irenaeus of Lyon said that "therefore did the Spirit of God descend upon him ... so that we, receiving from the abundance of his anointing, might be saved." The saint thus joins the presence of the Spirit in Jesus' flesh with the Spirit that he communicates to us. This is in fact the core element for us as priests and for Christian life within a theology of anointing: the same Spirit that animated and shaped Jesus' flesh has been transmitted to us, through this flesh of Jesus, as the Spirit of life. The Spirit is of the Father and of the Son, and it is given to us through the Son's flesh.

Now, we know that in our ordination as priests, and as deacons before that and, thereafter, as bishops, the Spirit is an element of the first importance in the prayers of consecration. The Spirit is made present in the laying on of hands—"he overshadows us" (see Lk 1:35)—because that shadow is the image of the Spirit. Thus our priestly ministry is exercised in the Spirit, under the inspiration of the Spirit. This will be understood in reading the texts of Saint Paul in which he places such emphasis on the fact that ours is a spiritual service, a ministry "in the Spirit" (see 2 Cor 3:6).

You also ask me about how a poor priest can become a conduit of the Spirit. Luther saw the priest as no more than the medium through which God spoke to us, and

he saw the sacrament as merely assigning his role to him
without really transforming him through grace. For us, the
sacrament is a transformative force that endows us with a
new identity in which the Holy Spirit can be poured out
in a new way. As priests, we are receptacles of the Spirit.
The Spirit enables us to represent Jesus: to become, with
him, a source of life for men. We are thus channels for
grace—sources, in a way, but always channeling from the
prime source, which is Christ.

Therefore, every priest, through the action of the
Spirit, becomes God's collaborator. We are instruments,
but living, animated instruments, who participate through
their freedom and creativity. The Second Vatican Council, in the dogmatic constitution *Lumen gentium* (no. 62),
expresses itself in these words:

> For no creature could ever be counted as equal with the
> Incarnate Word and Redeemer. Just as the priesthood of
> Christ is shared in various ways . . . , and as the one goodness
> of God is really communicated in different ways to His
> creatures, so also the unique mediation of the Redeemer
> does not exclude but rather gives rise to a manifold
> cooperation which is but a sharing in this one source.

We are "God's collaborators". It is the Spirit acting in
us, not our own merit, that makes us so; and we are God's
collaborators to the extent that we put ourselves at his dis-
posal, in obedience to his Word.

4. How can we participate in the being and work of Jesus?

*What nourishment does the priest give his congregation? Since
ancient times, divine pedagogy has shown man that it is not only,*

or even mainly, food that nourishes man, but rather the Word of God. When we consider the nourishment of doctrine, of the Word, we sometimes are seized by the idea that we must give people nourishment to prepare them; that otherwise they will not be able to digest it: Saint Paul speaks of feeding his flock with milk, as he would a child, or with solid food like an adult (see 1 Cor 3:2, Heb 5:12). On the other hand, however, the same food actually has enough nutritive strength to prepare people. How can the two things be combined?

There is a pedagogy for a priest when he addresses his congregation according to their human capacity and preparation. The priest, like a good pastor, a good teacher, should increasingly accommodate what his sheep can grasp according to their capabilities, at every step along the way. God also joined his people, the Israel of history, on their journey. He revealed the mysteries to them increasingly over time. Saint Irenaeus wrote some exquisite pages regarding the slow adjustment of God to men and men to God, until the coming of Christ. Jesus himself traveled a road with his disciples, little by little revealing to them the mystery of his Person. They did not understand, and the Lord opened their understanding little by little, with a fatherly patience and tenacity, so that they could comprehend.

But the logic of this pedagogical process is not purely human, of course, because it has to do with leading man to the level of a gift of God. The pedagogy of Israel did not involve simply a process of cultural maturation; rather, the figure of Jesus appeared at a certain point in history, shedding a new and unforeseen light on the whole process. The disciples received the Spirit, and only then did they attain the knowledge of the truth of Jesus. The priest should also bear in mind that God intervenes in the process of maturation, and so does grace, and that, as you say, the nourishment is potent, is in fact the main transformative force. We also know that this process is not just a gradual growth but, rather, demands a break with sin. The priest has to bear in mind, too, that Jesus calls us from death to life.

The priest ministers to his flock above all with two forms of nourishment: he serves at the table of the Word and also at that of the Eucharist, as the Second Vatican Council has so marvelously elaborated to us. With the Word and the sacrament, the priest is the father. And the pedagogical process that he must set in motion is realized in both.

Teaching faith, is that not a core task of the priest that is at risk of being lost, perhaps, among so many other chores and "activities"—bureaucratic, social welfare, economic? How does pastoral charity include a principle of unity in all the priest's activities, and how is light shed in all of them?

Faith is taught at several levels (before baptism, in catechism, and in theology, among others). A priest certainly has to be attentive to the means of transmission particular to each level, so as not to confuse them or neglect any of them, although he will probably be more attracted to and capable in one of them than in others. At each level, preaching develops according to its own logic, but without ever losing the integrity, the reference to the unity and holistic character of Christian faith, in the full transmission of the store of faith.

Regarding the risk that a priest will be distracted from his core duties by a certain excess of activity, I can certainly speak from my own experience, having had assignments that frequently developed at an intensely active pace.... We all run this risk, which exists and against which the Lord asks us to fight, this fast and furious pace that often deflects us from the essence of our calling. We must find time to take nourishment, to study and pray and thus nourish our preaching.

We must return to this traditional teaching of Saint John Paul II: "Being is more important than having or doing." Before he does this or that, a priest must "be"—that is, he must remember that his priesthood configures his persona with Christ. The most important thing of all is to nurture our "being priests", because missionary, apostolic action springs from this being. We could say that it wells up in our works, that the priest is like a glass that is filled with the Spirit and thence is poured out onto others.

Perhaps the priest also experiences a fear of teaching because he considers himself unworthy and a sinner, because he mistakenly thinks that the truth of his preaching depends entirely on the extent to which his life conforms to it. In that connection, I wanted to bring up the controversy between Donatus and Augustine of Hippo. Donatus argued emphatically that only holy priests could celebrate the sacraments. He based that argument on the Old Testament texts that say that the priest must be "unblemished". Saint Augustine expounds a different doctrine. He says, "Judas baptizes, Christ baptizes", meaning that the sinful priest also celebrates the sacraments correctly. Might this distinction not be useful to us sometimes in eliminating our complexes, our perplexities, and our fears when it comes to preaching the truth?

Well, what is involved here is the famous distinction between the act of a priest that is called *ex opere operato*—that is, which has effect regardless of the holiness of the priest—and what is called *ex opere operantis*—that is, which depends on how close the person who performs this action is to God. How are these two things related? I would make two points, looking at it in practical terms. First: *ex opere operato* gives us a certain existential peace and takes a great weight off us, because it tells us, "Look, although you are weak, this act is the Lord's, and it does not depend on you." That is a relief. This *ex opere operato*, as it was interpreted by the great medieval authors, means: "through the work wrought by Christ in his Passion and Resurrection". It is this work of Christ that counts, and we are its ministers.

But this is of course just one side of the coin. The priest cannot be satisfied with this. For he must know that, although God can always realize his work, the life of the priest is not immaterial to the spiritual fruit of his works. Therefore, precisely with respect to the spiritual fruit of his ministry, this desire to be personally close to Jesus Christ, through which we participate in the work of his Passion and Resurrection, bears so much fruit. Both things should always be present. These two points seem to me to be centrally important. A priest cannot content himself with *ex opere operato*. He must work to live what he preaches, to sanctify himself in sanctifying.

And, in this process, where should we begin? I would say: by acting like a priest when administering the sacraments. Because when the grace of Christ flows through us *ex opere operato*, we progressively become accustomed to it; we progressively learn how to shape ourselves with it in a way that will discipline our behavior.

You also mention fear, the priest's fear of speaking the truth. We referred to this before. It is true that the priest may succumb to fear of preaching because he sees himself as weak, but he can draw reassurance from a healthy humility and the thought that it is God who is acting in him. It is also helpful to remember what Saint Paul said in his First Letter to the Corinthians (1 Cor 3:6–7), that one plants, another waters, but it is God who gives the growth. This is a decisive principle in the life of an apostolic priest. It helps him to live his work with humility and to understand that he does not have control over everything, that the fruit depends on God, that the priest's role is to plant or water. And at the same time, it is a principle that extinguishes the fear of failure or of one's own limitations: our role is to play our part well, the watering or the planting, so that God can give the growth.

I do believe, on the other hand, that this fear of speaking the truth is a danger especially today. We need always to maintain a healthy balance, but the current difficulty may not be a strictness that demands too much from people but, rather, a letting go, a reluctance to get involved in problems. Our postmodernity is sometimes allergic to the truth, which can seem to be of no interest. That increases the temptation for us, too, to turn away from Christian truth, to speak only to feeling, to avoid posing the great choices of life to people.... The fact is that, without truth, man loses his way and his bearings, and he turns into a plaything with which others may serve their own interests. To proclaim Jesus' truth, which is the truth of his great love for man, is an especially important task for today's priest.

With a bit of exaggeration, certainly, but perhaps with an underlying truth, it is said that a spiritual father of a seminary used to tell his seminarians, "Preach the gospel; if you also live it, so much the better."

Well, there are some formulations that cannot be taken literally but that certainly have value for their underlying truth. The truth is that preaching is of a piece with living. The message should always be: "Preach the gospel and live it." But one may add to this message (and this is where the truth lies in the sentence you mentioned): "If in some circumstances you don't live it, don't stop preaching on that account; keep on preaching and struggling to right your life according to what you preach." This is the true part of the statement, which can help us because the paradox that it contains unblocks our moralism and helps us see a truth that we sometimes forget.

Where does a priest get his convictions of faith? What role does study play in this? And also, what role do teachers play in it?

The convictions of faith are learned above all in personal contact with the Lord. That is where they are acquired and strengthened. If we do not have this foundation, the convictions may be very deep and strong ..., but they may not constitute faith. Prayer, the pastoral life, study, deepening one's knowledge of theology, all of this must be in the service of personal contact with the Teacher, who is the fount of all Christian "conviction".

Could you cite three books that have particularly helped you acquire "Christian convictions"?

That is not easy to decide ... I would perhaps turn to the Christian classics. Leaving Scripture aside, of course, I think that among the books that have been most formative for me are *Adversus haereses*, by Irenaeus of Lyon, the *Treatise on the Trinity*, by Saint Hilary, and some of the subjects in the *Summa theologiae* of Saint Thomas Aquinas. These are three classic works in the great Christian tradition that resonate with me. As far as contemporary theologians are concerned, Father Congar and Father de Lubac would stand out, as would von Balthasar and Rahner in a different way. Congar and de Lubac were very directly inspired by the tradition and close study of the Church Fathers, and that has made them especially close and appealing to me. On the other hand, I have already mentioned how Father Orbe introduced me to reading the Church Fathers, and I would recommend his *Antropologia de San Ireneo*, a book that is full of fertile intuitions about man and his destiny in Christ, which underscores very well the importance in Christianity of the salvation of the flesh.

Finally, if you ask me for a more recent work of theology that has especially inspired me, I cannot fail to mention the three volumes of *Jesus of Nazareth* by Joseph Ratzinger, which have been a source of very significant theological and spiritual nourishment.

In literature, I unfortunately have less time to read now, but I would mention in particular the great authors, because one must always read the greats. The Spanish classics are always a source of nourishment: Cervantes and Calderón are always nourishing. The great Russian authors, such as Dostoyevsky, have also helped me (although I could not read them in Russian, unfortunately). I have drawn great nourishment from all of French literature, Camus, Bernanos, and others. And then there are the English novels, which have also interested me, such as Graham Greene's, among others.

5. When does Christ's Cross lose its relevance?

It sometimes seems as though Christian preaching has been "emptied", as though the Cross of Christ has been removed from it.

This happens when a dogma that is external to life is preached, or morality as an ideal, or an eschatology that is disconnected from the present. How should we respond to these three challenges of dogma, morality, and eschatology?

This is very important; this is fundamental. This is a crucial subject. There is no salvation that does not come through the Cross. That is what Saint Paul says, and we must say it: there is no path to salvation that does not pass through the Cross of Christ. All the saints have seen this. Perhaps it is difficult for us to accept it today, but it is a most important point. It has repercussions in morality, in spirituality, in dogma, and elsewhere. Without the Cross, we end up with a sweetened, impoverished, scrawny Christianity. This is a fact, and we must recognize it; we have let ourselves be somewhat carried away by the easy life, by consumerism, by the comfort of a "peaceful" life; on occasion, we have simply taken all of that as a given. And preaching, too, suffers from it.

Preaching the Cross is a stumbling block, as Saint Paul also said (1 Cor 1:23). And if it was a stumbling block for him, it is for us, as well. We tend to avoid it at times, reject it. It is, certainly, a challenge in our preaching of morality, which could come to be seen as a weight, as a kind of burden we have to carry; the true moral life, however, begins as a gift that we receive, which opens a horizon that is given to us to make our life greater. In one of his homilies, Pope Benedict XVI recalled the story of the pigeon and the cat, which is so instructive. When God created the pigeon, she did not have wings. She ran around back and forth on her fragile little legs and was easy prey for the cat. So she went to God to complain: "You have given me a clumsy body that is too heavy for my weak legs. This means I can never escape from the cat." God heard her plea and gave her wings. A few days later, though, the pigeon returned with her complaint: "Now you have thoroughly worsened my situation. You have added weight to my body with these wings, and now it is completely impossible for me to escape from the cat." Then God answered her: "You are a foolish animal. The wings are not a weight; they are precisely what will make it possible for you to fly and carry the weight of your body to save your life." Christian morality is not an added burden; it is precisely what enables us to fly and raise ourselves up.

You also mentioned the danger of living dogma as though it were something foreign to life. On that point, I would like to add that Christian faith has always nourished itself on the testimony of the martyrs, of the people in whom the Word of Jesus is put to the test and proven to be true: "Greater love has no man than this, that a man lay down his life" (Jn 15:13). Our current reality continues to be overrun with martyrs, with those who are giving their lives for the faith. Pope Francis puts great emphasis on this example of so many martyrs. These figures should be extraordinary exemplars for us because they show very clearly the relationship between doctrine and life. From them we can learn that doctrine is not something foreign to us, not an abstraction, but rather that it is something so important that we are willing to risk our lives for it. The martyrs should be for us the clearest expression of the fact that Christian faith is not an abstract ideal: it is a life, a specific path in which our entire life is at stake.

And regarding eschatology, yes, it has already begun. But we hope for more: that the Lord will fulfill his promise and that the seed he has given us will flower fully, so as to be all in us.

At other times, the Christian good news is sapped because it preaches Christ as Savior, which does not really resonate in man. That is, it does not proclaim the Christ who fulfills all that is human, who is the ultimate truth of creation. Might it be for fear that such preaching will make it difficult to have a dialogue with "the world"? For fear of being too radical in our approach?

We may have passed through a time when the gospel was preached as a burden. It was taken for granted socially, and man had to adapt himself to it. This approach is not productive today. If man does not see what it has to do with his desires, he will not want it. Preaching the gospel today therefore means demonstrating its attraction, and this requires showing how it opens us to the infinite mystery of God's love and mercy. This seems to me to be a decisive element on which we have already insisted: preaching a Christ who fulfills the human, a Christ who is truly the ultimate truth of creation.

It would be useful to distinguish the word "radical" (which derives from the word for going to the root) from "radicalization" or fundamentalism. Radicalism as such can lead to the most diverse deformations. In fact, we live today in a world that tends toward radicalization, in both the political sphere and the sphere of religion. Christianity is radical, in contrast, in being "love to the utmost", in recognition of divine mercy as it acts in the world. What can truly transform people and move them to conversion is this encounter. Let us recall the celebrated beginning of the encyclical *Deus caritas est*: "Being Christian is not the result of an ethical choice or a lofty idea, but the encounter with an event, a person, which gives life a new horizon and a decisive direction." It is this encounter that should be the core and the balance of a priest's preaching.

There is therefore an element of judgment in a priest's preaching that we must not forget. Christ certainly gives fullness to human nature and prompts us to give more of ourselves, but he does so precisely to the extent that, at the same time, he judges us and thereby cleanses and purifies us. Have we not perhaps lost some of the prophetic quality of preaching? Might it not be that we are trying to nourish the faithful with carob beans instead of bread from the Father's house? The Word, too, is medicine, and when we take it, our body is strengthened, like that of the prophet Elijah on the road to Mount Horeb. How can we really give manna, "the bread of heaven" (see Ps 78:24), in our preaching?

Of course: there is undeniably an element of "judgment" in preaching, because there are good things and bad in society. All the saints who have preached have made this distinction. It is about the work of discernment that is part of the priest's fatherhood. It is the great Christian subject of conversion, which reminds us of the need to turn and look at God in order to orient all things toward him.

I remember that in his encyclical *Spe salvi*, Benedict XVI spoke of the Last Judgment as a setting for hope. The pope explained beautifully how it is the expression of God's justice that at the end times will shine forth like light and that will give us reason to hope for evil's definitive destruction. Because the judgment that the priest renders is always a judgment for man's salvation, in search of healing.

There is a document of the International Theological Commission entitled *Theology Today* that concisely expresses the manner in which this judgment or discernment should be implemented in relation to the world. The document says that, in light of the gospel, one can better discern how the Spirit of God speaks through contemporaneous events. And it adds: "In all cases, *discernment must carefully distinguish between elements compatible with the Gospel and those contrary to it,* between positive contributions and ideological aspects, but the more acute understanding of the world that results cannot fail to prompt a more penetrating appreciation of Christ the Lord and of the Gospel since Christ is the Savior of the world" (emphasis added).

It therefore involves a dialogue that requires discernment—that is, a judgment—in order to attain a better understanding of how to promote and appreciate the truth of Christ, Savior of the world. In that discernment, it will be necessary to distinguish what should be promoted and encouraged from what should be purified. And all of this in light of the truth of Jesus, the truth of Christ, the Savior of the world.

6. Is theology pastoral?

The priest exercises his ministry of the Word in many different places and forms. An appreciation of these variations helps us communicate the Word more deeply and increase understanding of it. What words is it important for the priest to use in a homily, in his spiritual fatherhood, when he speaks to his congregation or in the confessional? What expressions are specific to each?

I would say, first of all, that it is not possible to create watertight compartments, that the priest should always bear in mind the integrity and totality of doctrine and Christian revelation as a whole. The truths of faith are like a body, and what affects one member affects all the others, as Saint Paul said.

In any case, it is indeed true that, when a priest preaches in his role as teacher, the Word is addressed to all, in a more universal way. He must take care, therefore, to maintain clarity in any exposition in which the truth of doctrine appears. In the confessional, on the other hand, he is more the priest as pastor, a guide of the soul, who speaks to a specific person and who therefore has before him that person's own problems and path to holiness. That is how, depending on which of these situations applies, one or the other role assumes greater prominence.

The most important criterion is at any rate given us by the gospel, and in the person of Jesus. In that sense, we see that, when the Lord is presented with the problem of divorce, there is a difference between the way he puts things in his dialogue with the Pharisees and the way he answers the Samaritan woman. In the first case, it was a matter of being clear in a public speech on an important question in which there was a serious cultural and religious obstacle to be overcome. There Jesus was unequivocal and clear in explaining the indissolubility of marriage and the hardness of heart that underlies divorce. In the second case, without in any way diminishing the same evangelical teaching, we see how the Teacher, in his dialogue with a specific person, the Samaritan woman, to whom he had to reveal where the difficulties in her life lay, took them on gradually, patiently, and calmly, with love, in an exercise of pedagogy, like a good shepherd who knows his sheep and knows how to bring them to the particular point in question. Whether it is a matter of a public reply or private accompaniment, the principle is the same, as is the goal to be attained, but the way of framing and conveying the Word differs. In any event, it is obviously crucial not to set the action of the pastor against that of the teacher. In one case as in the other, the unique truth of the gospel is what is being conveyed.

Who are the great figures in the history of the Church— particularly in the period of the Church Fathers that you know so well—who can help us understand the importance of doctrine and of a good education? Just as there are charismatic figures who teach us the value of prayer, of penitence, of apostolic courage, and more, where can we find figures who will help us illustrate the importance of knowledge of the truth?

I think we have many models in the history of the Church, though it may be more difficult to find them in modern times than it was in earlier days. There are of course the ancients, the great Church Fathers, like Saint Augustine or Saint Gregory the Great, and the great teachers of the Middle Ages, like Saint Bonaventure or Saint Thomas. There are many. I said that perhaps, among modern saints, we find the missionary, the shepherd of souls, the martyr, more than the theologian. But there is, for instance, the famous figure of Cardinal Newman. He is an exemplar of a saintly theologian, a man dedicated to teaching and knowledge of the truth. In him we discover that passion for the truth which led him to his conversion to Catholicism; and we discover, too, the passionate defense of conscience—not of a conscience that is prey to subjectivism, but rather a conscience that is the friend of truth—that allows it to be illuminated, taught, and purified through truth.

Can we say that there is no pastoral without the theological? There are those who think that time devoted to study belongs to the period of a priest's education, valid for an early stage of life or even something interesting, perhaps necessary for some, but in the end not relevant to pastoral work, to the day-to-day life of the parish and conversations with the faithful. Is that so? What pastoral imprint is there to be seen in theology?

Unquestionably, the pastoral cannot exist without theology. This is clear if we understand the study of theology to be the deepening of our understanding of God's Word. Obviously, a pastor's theological knowledge may vary in depth, but the pastoral has always had theology as its light. And it is necessary that it be guided by a good theology.

It should in any event be noted that there is a reciprocal nourishment, a relationship of reciprocity and circularity, between pastoral practice and theology. I have already referred to the great theologians, like Augustine of Hippo or Gregory the Great, who would never have attained the summit of theological thought to which they rose if they had not been pastors. Their pastorate gave them a greater depth, a more profound power of thought by which to grasp the reality of God. And I believe that the saints also illuminate another facet of this reality for us by showing us figures of simple people, like Thérèse of Lisieux, who, without having engaged in great study or read the great ecclesiastical writers, attained such knowledge of theology that the Church recognizes them as "Doctors". Hers is certainly an exceptional case, but it illuminates a reality of faith. There is indeed a profound relationship between theology and the pastoral, a close correlation between a life of faith and theological depth.

In that connection, it is also important to add that it is a gross error to separate "doctrine" from "the pastoral" as though there could be a pastoral truth or reality that lies outside doctrine or could somehow modify doctrine; as though doctrine could be relegated to a secondary level and we could distance ourselves from it. Theology would then be transformed into a game of doctrinal truths that, in practice, would be of little use. This is not and cannot be so, because theology and Christian doctrine are not a theory, not abstract reflections, aimed at establishing an assortment of general principles. They are the expression of the Christian life for the Christian life. A pastoral that is detached from doctrine loses its foundation. A pastoral that does not reflect on the truth of doctrine, with the help of theological thought, will also lose that foundation.

What advice would you give a young priest who has responded generously to the Lord's call but who views the world to which he will be sent with a certain fear and also views himself with the fear of inadequacy? And what would you say to an older priest who continues to work energetically in the Lord's vineyard, who is not lacking in faith, but whose hope for results may be beginning to falter?

Advice should be very concise and brief, so that is what mine will be. To the young priest: Trust in the Lord; to the older priest: Planting, not reaping, is the most important thing.

II

THE PRIEST AS FATHER
WHO PROPAGATES THROUGH
THE SACRAMENTS

A Conversation with
George Cardinal Pell,
Prefect of the Vatican Secretariat
for the Economy

1. A thread running through his own life:
A call to be *Pontifex*, Bridge Builder

Your Eminence, you will celebrate fifty years as a priest this coming December 2016. When you look back on those years in the priesthood, what do you see? I imagine you have had a wide variety of experiences, but if you had to define what a priest is, what would you say?

While the first duty of the priest is to preach the gospel of Jesus Christ, every priest is defined by the capacity to celebrate the sacraments. Especially the celebration of the Eucharist. Saint John Vianney explained the priesthood like this: "The priest continues the work of redemption on earth.... If we really understood the priest on earth, we would die not of fright but of love. The priesthood

Cardinal Pell's responses are taken from his original interview in English.

is the love of the heart of Jesus." This is not only put very beautifully, but it strikes our ears as strange. Many centuries earlier, with even greater eloquence, Saint John Chrysostom touched on these central mysteries. When celebrating the Eucharist, the priest should be transported to heaven, because with a naked soul and a pure mind, he is looking at heavenly things. He brings down, not fire, but the Holy Spirit, "to set alight the souls of all and make them appear brighter than silver refined in fire". The priest has to beg God to be merciful to all sinners, especially repentant sinners. Not only must the priest be able to sail his ship in fierce seas and resist the pirates trying to board his vessel, in order to build up the Church, but he must also remember that he has a power greater than that of the natural parents who bring us into this life. Priests bring us into the life to come; they can save the soul from spiritual sickness and, indeed, from spiritual death. Chrysostom put this, too, in a beautiful way: priests are more venerable than parents because they generate us to the life of God.

Every priest should be a *Pontifex*, a Bridge Builder, not just between people, but between God and his people. This is essential.

What are the most important gifts you have received in your life as a priest? What have been the most serious difficulties? I suppose that the fiftieth anniversary of your priesthood is also a moment of reflection about the road you have traveled, full of promises and fruitfulness. Which of these reflections can you share with us? In what has your priesthood been fruitful?

What have been the biggest difficulties for me? Well, for me, and for many of the priests of my generation, it has been the pedophilia crisis, having to defend how the

Church dealt with these matters, and also with personal accusations. One of the things of which I am proud is that I brought a new system of dealing with this; an independent investigator, making counseling available, making compensation available. We did this in '96 in Melbourne, which was six years before "Spotlight", the scandal in Boston.

What has been rich in my ministry? Well, that will be for others to judge, but I have taught regularly, trying to explain to people that God loves them, that Jesus is Redeemer and the Son of God, and also helping people with the sacrament of reconciliation, to receive God's pardon, after their personal repentance. I think that also I have tried to remind people of the four Last Things, heaven, hell, death, and judgment.

Certainly the moment of ordination was immensely powerful for me when I was ordained in Saint Peter's Basilica in 1966. I understood what I was receiving. So, while perhaps I did not always give sufficient emphasis to the sacrament of baptism, I have never underestimated the beauty and the importance and the grandeur of the priesthood.

Who are the priests who have had the strongest and deepest influence on your life? I am thinking not only of the priests of your childhood or youth, but also of those whom you have known during your ministry, your teachers in the art of priestly life, your guides on the paths of the ministry. Why have these priests had such a strong influence on you?

First of all, undoubtedly the most powerful influence on my priesthood was Pope John Paul II. I agree that he was one of the greatest popes in history; he was very much a priest and bishop; he was a poet; he had suffered enormously; one of the big messages from the life of John Paul II was the amount of suffering in his life that did not embitter him but purified him. His mother and his brother died early, as did his father. In his twenties he was alone. So he faced death and suffering continually in his life.

Also, John Paul II had a fine strategic mind; he saw the great issues of the age; he saw the struggle between secularism and the Church, with Communist and Nazi secularism, and with Western secularism. He was the greatest influence on my understanding of the priesthood.

When I was young, I was very much influenced by a priest who was chaplain of my secondary school. He was an intellectual, the first who introduced me to the Catholic intellectual tradition. He spoke to me about the role of the Church in the world, the role of laypeople, Catholic action, the action of Catholics. He was a most inspiring man. But, to my sadness, he left the priesthood. Later he became a very successful academic, a professor of history, who always remained committed to Christ and the Church.

I have worked with many good priests, and one such man was Father Frank Harman, priest, Roman canon lawyer, a "grey eminence", very wise, who gave me a lot of good and helpful advice.... But I have also worked with a number of laymen; the most important was a man called Sir Bernard Callinan, who had been a distinguished soldier in the Second World War. He was chairman of the board of our Institute of Catholic Education and a wise and strong man; so I learned much from him about the art of leadership and service, about strength and prudence and wisdom.

And during the age of Vatican II, what have been the most intense influences on the behavior of the priest and how he lives?

I was a student in Rome during that period (I stayed in Rome for four years). Some of my heroes during Vatican II were especially Father Henri de Lubac, with his *The Splendor of the Church*. Daniélou, too, was certainly one of my heroes. He had a great gift for explaining the faith of the Church to ordinary people. Yves Congar was profoundly important with respect to the role of the laity. His *Journal of the Council* is fascinating, brutally honest. Another man whom I met and listened to was Karl Rahner. I found his theological writings interesting, but they did not help me personally very much. However, his writings on spirituality were beautiful and very helpful to me; they were simple and eloquent and very faith-filled. In general, I found his method of theologizing very different from that of the English-speaking world.

A very good friend of mine, who did influence me a lot, going back to your earlier question, is a priest named Eric D'Arcy. He finished up as archbishop of Hobart; he was for twenty years a lecturer in philosophy at Melbourne University, and we regularly spoke about the importance of studying theology and being able to express theology in categories that would be accessible to English speakers. The thought patterns of a German like Rahner are completely different, so his work needs to be translated doubly, linguistically and conceptually. That certainly does not make his work less valuable, but it does make it less accessible to people in the English-speaking world.

I heard also Küng speaking during this time of the council, but I was never enthusiastic. I remember reading something of Chenu. And I wrote the minor thesis for my licentiate on Teilhard de Chardin. So I read everything of his that was published in the middle sixties. He was obviously controversial, but important for two reasons. First of all, for his attempt to reconcile theology and science, and also because he tried to integrate the theory of evolution with redemption history. And, of course, he was something of a mystic and a poet, so his book *La Messe sur le monde* is quite beautiful.

2. In what way is the priest a father?

A priest is also called a father. The key attribute of a father is that he engenders life and accompanies it as it flowers. I would like to ask you how, in your life as a priest, you have experienced the fatherhood that is part of being a priest. How have you lived it in your ministry? In what moments have you been able to see most clearly that a priest is a father?

Let me say something more general about this. The concept of paternity is absolutely central to Christianity, because Jesus called God his Father. He could have called God mother, but he did not. God could have come to us as a woman; but he did not. He came to redeem and to deliver us as a male, as the Son of his Father.

Hostility to fatherhood is partly explained by fathers who have been bad or inadequate to their children, especially to their sons; the relationship between fathers and sons is often a difficult one. In the famous novel by Ivan Turgenev, *Fathers and Sons*, this is clearly and dramatically explained.

But that is only part of the truth. For, since the beginning of modernity, there has been a general suspicion, antagonism to fatherhood, as if it were something that deprived us of freedom and autonomy. It is as if we wished to forget the fact that we have been born, that we come from another, that our life has been given to us, and by these ways to gain total independence. Gender ideology has to do with this, because it denies that the body has a meaning previous to our own willing and making. John Paul II said that the body is the witness that our existence is a gift. But we can understand this only through the experience of being born from a father and a mother.

It is clear that, after Freud, society has learned to kill the father. His role was too domineering, too closely linked to the idea of a rule that sets limits on a person. This is why Sartre said, "To beget children, nothing better; to have them, what iniquity!" The philosopher thought that the iniquity lay in the dependency that was established in the relationship between father and child. It is precisely in that respect that we can see that, along with the growth of feminism, the father has withdrawn and been absent, fading from the family. How does this affect the priest? The crisis of the priesthood is linked with a crisis in paternity. Nobody accepts paternalism today. How can the figure of the priest as father be regenerated today without falling into paternalism?

The views of Sartre and of Freud are deeply anti-Christian and, in many ways, anti-monotheistic. I visited the house of Freud in Vienna, and in his study, there were dozens and dozens of little images, I would say pagan images, semi-religious images. And I felt deeply uneasy there.

Undoubtedly, one of the roles of the father is to set limits, to maintain discipline, and not to be just a friend. The father is not a mother. And neither the father nor the mother should descend to sentimentalism. The father has to be a leader, the one who opens the way and points toward a great vocation.

Jesus was also someone who came to point the way; he was indeed the way. This is why, in his sacred humanity, Jesus is seen as our brother. Saint Paul speaks of Christ as the new Adam—that is, the new beginning. In his

sacred humanity, Jesus is the truest model and perfection
of humanity and, therefore, of genuine masculinity. In his
human nature, Jesus embodies all the human and especially
male qualities to perfection: as a warrior, he has come to
bring not merely peace, but the sword (Mt 10:34); forcibly
he removed the money changers from the temple when
they threatened by their behavior to desacralize it (Mk
11:15). As a father, he loves, especially the children, the
poor, the powerless, and the suffering. He has a word to
say that eliminates darkness and points the right way to
follow in life. He loved and loves sinners.

Now, the mystery of priesthood has to do precisely with
that: we represent Christ inasmuch as he is the head of the
Church, which means inasmuch as he is our brother and
leader. During the Mass, we say: "This is my Body", and
so we identify with Christ, who gave new life to the world.

One important role of a father is to indicate the true path
of life; he gives an example of sacrifice: when one knows
that there is a goal, a path toward fullness of life, one can
also bear the temptations and difficulties of the road. This is
the real mercy of the father, the mercy of pointing out the
way of salvation, the mercy of the prophet. The role of
the father is to lead, to inspire, and to correct, showing how
to treat everybody justly. So the father has to be able to say
"no", to define limits, to impose discipline, so that there is
space for love, so that there is order and space for growth.

And now—and this is very important—in the sacrament of reconciliation, we find a great expression of the
paternity of the priest as he forgives in Christ's name. By
helping people acknowledge their sins, the priest opens up
a path toward healing and hope, the true path of freedom.

I would also like to say two words about celibacy in
relation with fatherhood. For the Latin clergy, an essential
dimension of fatherhood is the priest's celibacy. Because

it means he is more easily able to be father to his whole community, a sign of spiritual paternity, a sign of universal love. Celibacy is in perfect accord with the essence of the priesthood and is a natural expression of this essence. Celibacy is a treasure for our Latin Church, not a burden. By thinking of celibacy in connection with fatherhood, we will see it, not only functionally, but as something that touches our identity as priests. Jesus' celibacy is a window to his relationship with his Father.

I also think that my own concept of paternity as a priest has developed slowly and over the years. I saw myself at the beginning as a brother with my brother priests, and only gradually did I think of myself more as a father. But certainly, right from the beginning, I regarded my priesthood, myself, as an *alter Christus*, as somebody called to personify what Christ is. Our fatherhood comes from the fatherhood of the one true God, and only if we remain one with Christ can we be true fathers.

Engendering man in accordance with God's plan: this is what the priest does as father. But the man of today is the man of late modernity, a man of whom it has been said that he lives between emotivism and utilitarianism. He is an emotive man, without deep and reasoned convictions, whose judgments in life are determined by the feelings he experiences. But he is also utilitarian in that he addresses life's problems in such a way as to promote his comfort and advantages. This is the man whom the priest addresses, encountering the difficulty of reaching his heart. Here is where temptation raises its head, the temptation to reduce the gospel to a sentimental message, concentrating wholly on love, but a content-free love, aimed at producing religious, benevolent feelings. How could this temptation pull the priest off the best pastoral path?

I think emotivism and sentimentalism are the greatest challenges facing the West. Turning back to your former question, this is the reason why many young men do not think of themselves as fathers at all.

For if we always follow our emotions, fatherhood seems impossible. How can I take responsibility for the life of another person if I am attached only to the fleeting moment? How can I teach this person that life consists of a great call and that happiness lies in answering this call, a call to love in its fullness? A love that is pure sentiment, a mercy that avoids the need for conversion, cannot be fruitful or educate, because it cannot endure and persevere; it cannot open up the path of life.

As a father, a priest is called to overcome this sentimentalism and to teach a love that is able to mature in time. True paternity is loving by being strong, by giving leadership. And the priest gives that leadership especially through the sacraments and his life and his teaching. Grace is like the sap that runs through the tree, like spiritual energy, like blood. In the sacraments, we have the love of Christ that endures, that is faithful, that accompanies us through life. In the sacraments, we learn that love means a new birth (baptism), that it can grow and be strengthened (confirmation), that it can be nurtured (Eucharist). A priest, when he prepares for the sacrament of marriage, teaches the youth that their love can say "forever", and in the sacrament of reconciliation, he teaches that this "forever" is possible because forgiveness is also possible.

Is the Western crisis of fatherhood part of the increased attraction of Islam? Islam offers a clear image of masculinity. Western males who have very little religion, no purpose, can be attracted in this sense even by extreme Islam and its violent camaraderie. For Catholics to capitulate to the whims of radical feminism on the truth of the father-hood of God would be not only doctrinally aberrant, but also strategically disastrous.

We can see today that Christianity is at risk of being reduced to its social utility. The socially acceptable image of the Church and of priests, as it is spread by the media, presents the priest as a man who embodies solidarity. The Church, the rites, God, have value to the extent that they promote this common solidarity. To what extent does this temptation constitute a risk for the priest?

A utilitarian concept of fatherhood is inadequate. It is useful for whom? For the father? For the mother? Or for the children? Is he only a father because he wants to have children? Do the children think the father is useful because he gives them food and shelter? The father is much more than something useful, as are the children. The father with his wife are for the children the memory of their origin; father and mother point the way to their children's vocation; they teach them sacrifice and self-gift, true love.

Some priests are too much concerned about being useful for society. And it is true that a priest needs to enrich the life of the people in practical ways, like teaching children and helping the poor and bringing reconciliation to families, and this is very good and necessary. But the most important task of the priest is to point to God, the source of love, the reason for our faith and hope, God as the beginning and end of everything.

If the priest is busy only doing all things that are useful but forgets what is essential, what truly determines his identity, his life will finish in frustration or emptiness. For being a father is not something the priest does, but something the priest is.

The so-called new models of "shared ministry" can serve to obscure this identity. The priest could be seen no longer as a father but as another member of the "pastoral team". The paternity of the priest must be compatible with a genuine collegial model that is truly collaborative, where everyone possesses a unique identity and role. But competing with this is the liberal democratic model that seeks to be purely egalitarian, where everyone's role is equal and often undifferentiated and where, therefore, personal identity is blurred. So some tend to clericalize the laity, while the priest is secularized.

Your Eminence, you have devoted so many years of your life as a priest to the study of theology, and then of education, philosophy, history, and more. Why is education and a profound understanding of doctrine so important for a priest? I am thinking, first, not just of its utility as a contribution to incisive preaching, but above all of its value for the priest himself; does he really put some of his being on the line in deepening his knowledge of history and doctrine? Can a priest be a priest if he does not have a light by which to illuminate life, society, and history?

Look, I am completely at one with John Paul II on the importance of "ideas", on the struggle in society between secularism and Christianity as two concepts of being human. "Ideas" are enormously important for priests. I remember a bishop once saying to me that his young priests had not studied philosophy; so they had a great difficulty in understanding what the office of priesthood was, because they thought of it simply as a collection of functions, not as something that changes the very being of the person. So I am strongly convinced that the greatness of the priesthood, its human and spiritual contribution, is based, initially at least, on the study of philosophy. A good philosophical training means that a priest is able to analyze an argument, is able to put together a synthesis on what way we should go forward. And priests and especially bishops need to be strategists, who can see the bigger picture, who try to see the future and then can decide what needs to be done today so we can go on toward Christ's goals.

Formation is necessary also because the secret of Christian vitality comes from Christ. We are Christians. So all the reform movements in the Church are based on a *resourcement*, on a return to the sources (*fontes*). Thus we need a profound knowledge of the basic tradition and of the Scriptures.

Another important issue is the knowledge of history, because many periods have been difficult in the history of the Church. Some of them have been marvelous, but there is always a tendency, a temptation, to think that the difficulties of our time are unique, that the Church has never had problems like this in the past. History gives us a wonderful sense of perspective, an antidote to pessimism.

Karl Barth, a great Protestant theologian of the middle of the twentieth century, said that when you are writing a sermon, you need the Gospel, on one hand, and the newspaper, on the other. And there is some truth to that. But a Catholic would say that you need not just the Gospels but also the *Catechism of the Catholic Church*, which is a compendium of what we believe. The importance of formation increases as the life of the priest goes on.

Perhaps a fundamental issue in the education of a priest is the nature of morality. Are there moral truths? It is important for priests to be trained in moral philosophy (especially in the virtue theories of Aristotle and Thomas Aquinas). We cannot decide to define morality according to personal tastes. Society would collapse from radical individualism. A compass or a watch has to be property calibrated.

There are moral truths just like there are truths of health. If we smoke too much or we drink too much alcohol, this damages our health, and so if we tell lies and are selfish, our moral life is damaged. One of the great battlegrounds today in the Western world touches on sexuality, marriage, family life. Many people live in family situations that are radically imperfect. And we need to teach that God's forgiveness is so great that the hearts of people can be changed and can come out of sin.

Perhaps the philosopher Charles Taylor's idea about the concept of secularization will be helpful in understanding that need. A priest who does not understand this concept may be able to do many things, but he will not bear fruit. There are three levels of secularization: the first, which is the most immediate, consists of a reduction of religious practice; the second is that of a Christianity that no longer has an influence in society or in culture; and, on the third and most dangerous level, faith becomes a choice that no longer has an influence on one's own identity. If the priest aims his efforts at one of these levels without taking the underlying problem into account, he will be like a physician who cures symptoms without taking the source of the virus into account. How, in the end, does distinguishing among these three levels help the priest?

I was for years at the University of Oxford, where I came to understand more the strengths of the agnostic position. My father was not a Catholic; he was a nominal Anglican. He was religiously tone deaf. So I have always understood people who have little religious feeling or understanding. This has been very helpful to me, but only because I have continued to study the Catholic tradition as the key to understanding modern life.

Many Catholics, especially in the English-speaking world, overestimate the extent of secularism. In the Western world, we celebrate Christmas and Easter, we celebrate Sundays, many people are still influenced by Christian notions of universal love and human rights. You can understand this without a Christian background. And, of course, we know that in the depth of the human heart, God continues to call every single person to a fullness of life, and this gives us hope.

Having said that, we must admit that secularism has made enormous progress. So it is not enough to help the individual to have an experience of God, but we need to build a Christian culture, an environment in which one can breathe. It is very important for this that the priest understands his own tradition, the Catholic tradition, which is based upon the sacraments and upon concrete practices of life: prayer, work, family ... And if he knows his own tradition and is able to live it and to propose it to his parishioners, he will adapt and give appropriate answers.

I have enjoyed very much reading a book by M. Eberstadt, *Adam and Eve after the Pill*. In this quite little book, Eberstadt explains the sociological consequences of the invention of the pill. It has changed, not just the number of children, but a whole world of thinking, the role of men, the role of women, marriages ... A priest needs to be aware that secularization affects not only the individual, but the culture, our ways of living together.

3. Is the priest a man for others?

Your answer has to be viewed today in the light of a new development that distinguishes the times we live in from the past: we do not have enough priests, and the faithful continue to demand liturgical services in their parishes. The priest is seen today as a

provider of services, who must attend to religious needs, rituals,
or solidarity with the congregation without being able to devote
himself to what he would consider to be more fruitful. A pastorate
that is called sacramentalist has thus developed, in which the priest
becomes above all a dispenser of sacraments. Is this a valid criti-
cism, or do such comments conceal an even deeper difficulty than
the lack of time—that is, a difficulty concerning the true meaning
of the priest's ministry?

The difficulty is much more profound, much more widespread. And I think it is connected with the decline of
many of the religious orders, because they were centers
of spiritual vitality that fed the religious lives of people
who came to Mass. The priest cannot do everything by
himself; he needs laypeople. Laypeople are called to became active participants. Not necessarily paid laypeople,
but volunteers, active parish leaders. We need this joint
effort to pass the faith to the next generation. If there is no
community, then the priest is just always giving the "last
rites", sacraments to a dying Church.

Also, many of our parishes no longer provide for the
young people an adequate sociological defense. Many
times they are swept away by society. For example, people say Catholicism is anti-sex or anti-progress, and young
people need arguments, and they need structures to
be protected. It is important to develop these institutions.

So I think it is no surprise that in Spain 40 percent of
churchgoers belong either to the Neocatechumenal Way or
to Opus Dei. Both of them have institutions, community-
life practices that defend young people and help the
transmission of faith. I did not realize until fairly recently
the significance of the Neocatechumenals' celebration of the
Eucharist on Saturday night. When the young members are
at Mass, they are not at the nightclubs and especially, as in

some Roman parishes with fifteen or twenty communities, they can create their own community together afterward.

One of the good things I did in Sydney was to set up teams of laypeople, chaplaincy teams, in state universities, following the Evangelical-Anglicans in Sydney and of course the FOCUS groups in the United States. One of the big changes in the last twenty or thirty years in the United States is the activity of chaplains and groups at the secular university. So, when I came to Sydney, at Sydney University there were probably eight thousand Catholics, twenty of them in the chaplaincy. Now the numbers are not enormous, but there are hundreds and hundreds. And in fifteen years of the new university chaplaincies in Sydney, fifty-two people have entered to become priests or nuns. So, you might say fifty-two is not an enormous number, but it is much, much bigger than it was. I am sure this is a key strategy, in Australia at least.

Among the services that priests must provide, one that has become a greater burden today is the administration of the parish. Bureaucratic and financial matters have grown notably more complicated. A great part of the priest's time and energy is therefore devoted to such matters, which are not directly religious. Are these matters important? Is there not a danger that the priest is being reduced to being a religious functionary? What is at stake in these administrative duties? In asking this question, I am fully aware that I am posing it to a priest who is the prefect of the dicastery charged with the Vatican's economic affairs.

It might be that the answer to this question differs from culture to culture. Because there are some priests, especially in the English-speaking world, who are more practical, who very much like this as a part of their ministry.

But obviously it is easier to organize the parish finances than to convert someone. The priest, as I said, has to be a *Pontifex*, a Bridge Builder, to the Transcendent, not just a bureaucrat. I think it was Eugène de Mazenod, founder of the Oblates of Mary Immaculate, who said that it is not impossible for a priest to live like a practical agnostic. And I think that is right.

Let me put to you another example of this. Some people, when they do not know what to do, spiritually or religiously or as a priest, set up a committee, or they organize an office, or they write a plan. Sometimes planning for the future can be an escape from having to do something today. I remember being called to comment on the pastoral plan of a group of nuns. It was very complicated, sophisticated planning. I would say it was like the plans of Napoleon to invade Russia! And then, at the end of my work, I discovered they had only fifteen active nuns.

Yes, it is true, in order to solve pastoral problems, sometimes commissions are established and elaborate pastoral plans are drawn up. Alasdair MacIntyre has been critical of the fact that in our society, which has given up the search for the common good of all men, it is the manager *who has emerged as the great figure. That is, the figure who seems to be capable of efficiently managing the attainment of all the various goals everyone is pursuing. Is the priest at risk of becoming a* manager *of the community—namely, a "spiritual* manager*", who offers a variety of services to its members to ease their consciences, but without furthering the great life of communion? How can this risk be avoided?*

Each priest labors in the light of eternity, calling believers and others to eternal life. He calls people to faith in God and moral conversion. It helps when a priest is a good manager, when a bishop is farsighted and strategic, but such planning and administration must be God-centered, inspired by Christian hope, and not used as an escape from, or alternative to, genuine religion. The priest must be more than a manager of the here and now; he must be a leader calling his followers to God and eternity.

In the ambit of civil society, saying that a priest is a "man for others" can seem like a way of presenting a more acceptable, kinder figure, who fills a greater need in a society in which there are so many solitary people who require spiritual help.... But is this enough? This living for others, this "pro-existence": What is its source? Would it not be better to say that the priest is called to live "for God", or, more specifically, "for the Eucharist", inasmuch as he is a priest for the Eucharist and for all it signifies? It is true that the priest is called to offer the Eucharist and all it implies to others, but what is the decisive point at which his specific path to holiness is at issue? What is the unifying principle of a priest's life?

The priest is a man who lives in the Spirit of God. Especially in the English-speaking world, people can become deaf to spiritual realities, and the priest is there to remind them of the reality of the Spirit. I used to go out before confirmations, when I was assistant bishop, and speak to every class I was confirming. I used to speak to them for an hour, asking questions. At the age of twelve or thirteen, students were happy to answer. I would ask them: What is God like? What is God made of? What is "spirit"? Many of them could not say anything about "spirit". Now that we have changed the translation in the English liturgy to "The Lord be with you—And with your spirit", they have to come across the word "spirit"; they have to think about it a little bit. So, in every class I went to, after that, I spoke about God as Spirit: God is spiritual; God is Transcendence; God is love. To say that God is Spirit is not to say that he is ethereal, alien to everyday life, or that he acts only in the realm of interiority, but not in the concrete circumstances of our lives. To the contrary, Spirit means God's presence in the middle of the world. God is Spirit means that he is real, powerful, and invisible—a bit like gravity or electricity but personal and able to love. So if the priest is a man of the Spirit, he is at the service of this breath of God, who gives life to us and moves the whole world.

I am a great believer in "crucifixion Christianity". We could say that the priest is attached to the Cross, and thus he is an expert in knowing the suffering of his people and explains this suffering as a path toward God. Paul never founded a community in Athens. He was unable to. Why? Well, when he spoke to the Athenians in the agora, he never mentioned the crucifixion. But after that, when he went to Corinth, he certainly did not make the same mistake: he spoke about crucifixion and about Christ's redeeming love on the Cross. And he founded there a lively community.

The priest is a man of the Spirit as a man of the Cross if he is a man of the Eucharist. It is the Eucharist that gives meaning to all he does. And, in the Eucharist, he understands that, for all his giving, there is Someone who has given more than he has. Before being a man for others, he understands that he is a man *from* God, a man *from* Christ's love, and this encourages and sustains him during all his ministry.

4. Is sacramentality a kind of sacramentalism?

What does celebrating the sacraments signify? One of the great issues in the debate between Donatus and Augustine was precisely the subject of the priesthood and the significance of the sacraments that the priest celebrates. Donatus said that the priest confers grace in proportion to his holiness. Augustine countered with the great ecclesial vision: the grace the priest ministers is God's. I think this might be helpful to us in overcoming an excessively moralistic view of the priest, a view in which the main thing asked of him is that he be a "good person". But might not the mystery of the priesthood be lost in an excessively simplistic view? What does it mean to say that the priest is called to "administer the mysteries of God"?

Early on I learned the distinction between *ex opere operato* and *ex opere operantis*, and about the validity of the sacraments even with a sinful priest. And of course I accept that completely. It allows us to understand that we are instruments, that eternal life comes not from us, but from God.

On the other hand, this does not mean that the participation of the priest is not part of the sacrament. Saint Thomas says he is also an instrument of the communication of grace, a living instrument. So if the priest does not prepare his sermons, if he celebrates without respect, he is destroying the faith of the people. And if he celebrates with devotion, he is sanctified by the administration of the sacraments and God can transmit better the grace of the sacrament through him. So there is a correlation between genuine liturgy and the faith of the priest.

I think it is no coincidence that in many places such as Belgium or Holland, very secularized countries, priests do not use the approved Eucharistic Prayers. As Pope Benedict pointed out: bad liturgy is destructive of Catholic life. The Church is born from prayerful, devout Eucharists. The Eucharist is not just a community celebration centered on the priest.

The sacraments are linked with the transformation of individuals and their relationships because they introduce us into the life and Body of Jesus. By entering into Jesus' Body, we enter into God's original plan. This means, therefore, that the sacraments regenerate God's original plan in our body, our relationships, which we live in our body. In effect, the sacraments transport us back to creation. But how does this transformation come about? How is the priest a father through the sacraments? What does baptism regenerate in the believer?

Your question shows that the mission of a priest cannot be lived in isolation. He needs to build a community with a Christian culture; he needs laypeople, lay leadership, lay servers. The sacraments are a great gift from Christ that allow precisely that. The sacraments are not only gifts for the individual, but they create relationships, they generate communion. So in baptism, we are incorporated into the Church; in confession, we receive reconciliation with Christ and with his Body; in the Eucharist, a new people is generated in charity ... I think this is very important for our priesthood. We are not called just to foster individuals in their isolated path to God, but we are called to nurture relationships. So when we look to a parishioner, we need to think: This is not just an individual; this is a person who lives in relationship with others: with parents, wife, husband, brothers, children ... Because only if these relationships grow can this person find God and find fulfillment in his life. And the sacraments are one key to this.

"The priest of the next millennium, if there are to be any priests, will be a mystic." This apothegm expresses a thought that is very current today: mysticism, the inner way, appears in the guise of the solution to the problems of our Christianity. I would like to

propose a different expression: "The priest of the next millennium, if there are to be any priests, will be sacramental." I am trying to convey with this new version the necessity of insisting on the sacramentality of Christian life. In the sacraments, grace is communicated precisely through visible acts, which link us to others and assume a world that is created in its concreteness and also generates human culture. We priests need to be introduced anew into this sacramentality of Christian experience. Do you think this diagnosis is accurate?

Mystics are rare. Not every, perhaps not many priests will be mystics. I do not accept this ideal of just a few brave middle-class Christians. One of the strongest traditions in the Catholic Church is popular religion. I hope more and more of the priests will be mystics. But even if they are not mystics, they can still be good priests. The Spaniards had a genius for propagating popular religion in the Americas and Philippines. Pope Francis is also very much engaged with this popular faith. So am I. And I do not need to be a "mystic" to do that.

So I think in the Western world, the alternatives are the model from the United States or the model from Germany and the low countries, Holland, Belgium. And the model from Germany is dying. Now what is the model from the United States? I think it recognizes that vitality comes from following Christ and accepting his teachings, given to us in the Catholic tradition. Too many are tempted to think that we will make better progress by modernizing, by adapting to the secular world. This would be catastrophic. We do not need to guess about the consequences of this liberal model. We have seen them in our Catholic Church: in Belgium, Holland, Quebec, and we see them in the liberal Protestant churches. They are disappearing.

So, for example, to think that you will increase the number of Catholics by allowing a few people to go to Communion after they are divorced and remarried is bizarre. Progress in Christianity comes from people embracing the cross. And through the cross you come to redemption and rejoicing and resurrection. Jesus did not have only success when he preached the gospel; he was rejected and crucified and assured us that the world would hate us. By preaching and accepting the cross, by our Christian witness of charity and forgiveness, this is the way to bring salvation to the world and come to the resurrection.

So the Christian of the future, as you said, must be "sacramental", must have a sacramental dimension. If there is no sacramental dimension, we do not have the Catholic Church. So, for example, without holy ordination and matrimony, there is no Catholic Church. The idea of "sacramentality" will be central for our future Church, as it has always been central. Because the sacraments bring the grace of God to the people, and it is in the sacraments, especially in the Eucharist, that we worship God.

Only through baptism can we be sure that children became children of God. Only through the sacrament of reconciliation can we be sure that God forgives.

5. What purpose do creative minorities serve?

You have studied the philosophy of history, Your Eminence, and you know Toynbee's theories very well. This historian has shown how, in the course of history, decisive moments of change have seen the emergence of "creative minorities" that are capable of generating new life-styles in a context that challenges the culture lived theretofore—minorities that are capable of responding to an era's new challenges in a new and creative way. Could Toynbee's theory be a response, on a historical level, to what the Lord says in the Gospels in the parables of the little flock, of the yeast, or of the salt? So when we speak of creative minorities, do we not suggest a way for us, as priests, to do our work as pastors? Should we, too, not take "creative minorities" as a model for our work in evangelization, precisely as the Christian modality for reaching out to everyone? If this is true, what consequences do you see for the work of the priest?

Toynbee's idea, taken up by Pope Benedict XVI, can be very fruitful today. Always, in any movement, in any realm, there are only a limited number of people who will provide leadership. Some sociologists say: If you have 16 percent of any group, that is a creative minority sufficient to change the whole group. For Toynbee, a creative minority is the one that is able to create culture, a way of being together, of working, having leisure.

In the past, the religious orders provided these creative minorities. Nowadays, these creative minorities are found also in what I call the "new movements". So this is a providential instrument of God: Opus Dei, charismatic groups, the Neocatechumenal Way, groups like Emmanuel, Focolare … Another example of creative minorities are the FOCUS groups in the universities in the United States. Another example of a creative minority is the small liberal arts college, such as Thomas Aquinas College in the United States, Campion College in Sydney, Australia.

These can be the creative agencies of our future. And, of course, there are Christian families, a great creative minority. As a bishop, one important criterion for me was whether each group could pass on the faith to most of their children.

The problem for Christianity is not only to empower individuals, but to generate a Christian culture. And this is precisely what is becoming more difficult today. If we are no longer able to talk about what a father or a mother is or about the meaning of the body, it is impossible to profess our faith in Jesus Christ, in his Incarnation, in his revelation of God the Father. The cultural struggle is real. It was started, not by us, but by people who want to destroy faith, Christian marriage, destroy the Christian concept of family and of sexuality and of the value of life. It is important to be aware of this in order to understand how, as priests, we can enlighten people and help them live their lives in fullness.

Of course, a creative minority is not a ghetto. It is crucial that the creative minorities realize that they exist to serve everyone, not just themselves or their friends. They are there to serve the whole Catholic community and society.

It is essential for a priest who wants to work within this logic of "creative minorities" to be capable of "generating environments" in which it is possible to live sacramentally. That is, to generate spaces in which it will not be a miracle to live as a Christian, in which the Christian life will be abetted by social mediations, in which the Christian act will not be radically countercultural. Perhaps the underlying question is how to generate a Christian culture.

Well, the individual priest is limited in what he can do. This is why he has to work with his community. If he belongs to a creative minority, he needs to cultivate his own relationships, with his bishop, his brother priests, his parishioners ... And he must try to educate and develop his community. To create a Christian culture, he needs educated Christians. This is also why I insisted on the need for educated priests who know the Catholic tradition.

We have many Catholic schools in Australia, which educate 20 percent of all Australians. Some people, serious international people, think it is the best Catholic school system in the world. But, unfortunately, its religious influence is limited. Moreover, some people fear and think that in fact some schools are inoculating the students against real Christianity. They reduce Christianity to limited things: you are kind, you take care of social justice, you celebrate Christmas and Easter ... but not too much about commitment and repentance and not too much "crucifixion Christianity". When we put faith at the center, we can help adults to flourish, become more human. When we put our faith aside, education becomes only a technical preparation or a socialization of people, which puts aside the question of the meaning of life and the meaning of society, of the reality of God.

We have talked before about the sacramentalist pastorate, which concentrates solely on the administration of the sacraments. We now have a better understanding that what that actually means is a sacramental pastorate, the central point of which is to regenerate the individual by also regenerating his relationships and the environments in which he lives. The Church's tradition has seen this as the development of gifts received in the sacraments and thus has shaped an entire "mystagogy"—that is, the way sacramental logic sets us on a path that has to be explained later, little by little, in the community of faith. The Church Fathers, like Saint Cyril of Jerusalem in his Catechesis, *initiated this mystagogy after the sacraments, not before. The sacrament was therefore not just a destination but the capacity to create a new path. Is "mystagogy" a path for priests? How can it be made truly traversable?*

We know that the preparation for the sacraments is very important, and the Church has invested a lot in it. Certainly, the sacraments are not only the end of a path but also, and more importantly, the beginning. In the sacraments, we receive a gift, a gift that must be taken care of and fostered, so that it produces fruit, as the Lord says in the parable of the talents. In this sense, I do think it is important to recover the idea of mystagogy. This is one of the strengths of the Neocatechumenal Way: they offer concrete practices that accompany the people in community.

6. How can the priest be a companion on the path opened by the sacraments?

I would like to consider your response in the context of three specific sacraments. The first is the sacrament of the Eucharist and preparation for First Communion. The Church makes a great effort to prepare children for their First Communion. Ever since the days of Pius X, there has been a monumental educational effort. Even so, and much to the surprise of priests today, they see that First Communion sometimes ends up being the only one, leading nowhere, because the children never set foot in church again. This obviously stems from the fact that their families do not accompany them. But I think today's priest should address the preparation for First Communion precisely through the lens of mystagogy: What paths should be followed after First Communion?

The mystagogy, as the Fathers practiced it, was an introduction to the mystery of Christ, to his salvation. It is interesting that it took place after the celebration of the sacraments of Christian initiation. In this way, it was clear that the explanation followed the experience of the encounter with Christ; it was not only a theory, but the truth of the new life the Christians were already living.

Can we apply these thoughts to First Communion? Of course, there has to be a preparation for First Communion;

it has to be received in a worthy way. More often in past times, children who received Communion had a path before them, to deepen their faith, going to Mass with their families. Today, however, we cannot take this for granted. This situation demands of us a change in mentality: instead of investing all our energies in preparation, it would be useful to encourage, in our schools and parishes, a catechesis that follows First Communion, that helps the children, and the rest of the families, understand the implications of the gift they have received. This is a big challenge, but it is attempted in good parishes and the new movements.

The second sacrament I would like to address is confirmation. There is here a very disconcerting problem. Some have compared confirmation with receiving an academic degree: once it is granted, you bid the recipient farewell and never see him again. How can we promote, above all, a mystagogy of the sacrament of confirmation that will encourage a person's later development?

We have got to explain to the people that confirmation is not like a graduation; it cannot mean that we never see you again until you want to get married. You are confirmed; you can now go out and live a kind life all by yourself. But this is not the Christian view of the sacrament.

The challenges and obstacles to Christian living are clear and formidable for our young people. The answers are not always clear, but they are usually difficult as they involve faith and sacrificial love.

I would like to ask, too, how we can pose today the great question of the priest's vocation as it relates to celibacy.

I am glad you mention celibacy, because that is an important area. Jesus was celibate. Paul was celibate. And Jesus spoke of those who are eunuchs for the Kingdom. So it is a New Testament idea; and it frees people for service, for work. It is also a very powerful sign or symbol of the importance and the reality of the supernatural. Priests do not become celibate because marriage is bad; rather, they choose celibacy recognizing that they are sacrificing something that is good and beautiful and vital: natural marriage. Moreover, by choosing celibacy, the priest brings to fulfillment the vocation to self-giving and fruitfulness that is implied in marriage. Celibacy is not to remain alone; rather, it means a total consecration to God in Christ and to the Church.

It also brings some "practical" advantages; of course, they are not the main point, but it is good to remember them: it is much cheaper for the Church and for the communities to have a celibate clergy. In many ways, the celibate priest can be classless; he does not have a wife from a certain class; his children did not go to a certain class of school. In my ministry, I have been in some of the wealthiest homes in my parish and some of the poorest homes, and I was welcome in both of them. Priests are able to travel to new areas of work. A pope does not have to ask his wife if she would like to live in Rome!

Historically, the Catholic faithful have always had an instinctive perception of the self-sacrificing and disinterested love represented by the celibate priest. We find confirmation of this from an unlikely source (F. Nietzsche, *Die Fröhliche Wissenschaft*, no. 358):

> Today we see clearly that Luther was fatally limited, superficial and imprudent.... He gave back sexual intercourse to the priest: but three-quarters of the reverence of which

the people are capable (and particularly the women of the people) rests on the belief that a man who is exceptional in this regard will also be exceptional in other matters. It is precisely here that the popular belief in something super-human in man, in the miraculous, in the saving God in man, has its most subtle and suggestive advocate. Having given the priest a wife, he had to take from him auricular confession. Psychologically this was appropriate, but thereby he practically did away with the Christian priest himself, whose profoundest utility has ever consisted in being a sacred ear, a silent well, a grave for secrets.

Obviously, to say that celibacy belongs to the essence of priesthood can imply disrespect for married clergy in other Catholic rites. You cannot say that celibacy is the essence of the ministerial priesthood, but it is an appropriate expression of the ministerial priesthood, because we follow the example of Christ and the examples of Paul and John.

The third sacrament on which I would like to ask you to shed some light is that of marriage. Experts say that most divorces happen in the first years of marriage. The Church makes a great effort to prepare couples who want to marry, but what does she do thereafter? Would it not be best to concentrate creatively on how to accompany couples? I am thinking, for example, of the birth of the first child, a very gratifying moment but also one of great uncertainty in the couple's life. I also am thinking of the need to shape a good relationship between family and work or to foster conditions favorable to the forgiveness of offenses. How can the Church have a presence in these beautiful but difficult years?

Well, we turn back to the question of taking care of the gift received in the sacrament. We have invested some resources in the preparation for marriage, and I do not think this has always been effective. The real problems of married life usually do not appear before marriage; they usually occur after the wedding, especially during the first years of married life. We cannot assume, as was the case some decades ago, that the spouses are being supported by their extended family or by society. Good parish communities can help those in difficulty. In many ways, community, friends, and fellow believers are better placed to support and help these couples than a priest. Of course the priest has his mission in encouraging and helping, but he cannot be everywhere and do everything. Diocesan programs to help married couples in difficulty can often bear fruit.

The key point is always the same: the sacrament is not a point of arrival but a point of departure. It is important that spouses remember something we have forgotten in our society: that marriage is not a question of two; rather, it is a call to be at the service of the common good, enriching the life of society by the creation and education of children.

These specifics regarding priestly work face a new difficulty today: when the priest speaks on the gospel of marriage, he sometimes encounters people who not only live a contrary life; they do not even want to live according to that gospel, and yet they have great religious feeling. The difficulty arises when they propose to live a sacramental life but do not want to change their conduct; and the media provide them with justification for their intentions, so they demand that the priest administer the sacraments to them. It pains me to see that today's priest is fearful of his parishioners precisely for this reason. What would you say to a priest who finds himself in this situation?

The priest has to explain these things clearly to people in irregular situations: they can still pray, still come to the Holy Mass, hear the Word of God ..., but they are called to work toward repentance and toward the acceptance of Christ's words. We have no authority to reverse the teaching of Christ, which brings to fulfillment our desire to love.

We follow Jesus Christ, we follow the Catholic teaching. With love and sensitivity we have to help people to the truth.

In *Amoris laetitia,* it is clear that Pope Francis did not have the intention of changing Church doctrine by a footnote. The teaching of Saint John Paul II and of Benedict XVI has been very clear regarding the impossibility of admitting to Holy Communion someone whose way of life contradicts the indissolubility of marriage. Even in the internal forum, conscience is at the service of truth, and good confessors recognize this.

Naturally we can have genuine developments in doctrine, but Church teaching cannot be turned on its head.

The Priest, a Spouse *is the title of a recently published book. In this short book, that term leads precisely to an understanding of the Church as Bride. It thus is understood that the priest's vocation looks not to the isolated individual but to the community; not only must he foster the lives of specific individuals, but he must also bring individuals into a communion and enrich that communion. Faced with a society like ours, which is radically individualistic, in which everything is measured in terms of the individual in isolation, how can the priest be a spouse, which bespeaks a new logic, the logic of the Body of Christ: the Church and her members?*

Well, Christianity means community. The priest is there for the community, and he is representing Christ as the

Bridegroom of this Church. I would like to mention in this sense one detail. I heard a beautiful lecture from a Jewish convert where she explained the meaning of the baldachino, the four columns and covering over the altar in some first-millennium churches in the West, especially the famous baldachino in Saint Peter's, Rome. The baldachino comes from the veil that in the Jewish wedding ceremony is held over the bride and groom when they are making their promises to each other. So this baldachino over the altar is a sign of the marriage between Christ and the Church.

The Italian writer Susanna Tamaro has given one of her novels the provocative title Forever. *The novel aspires to answer the great question whether "forever" exists or not, and its answer is clear: "forever" is all that exists. In so saying, it explains what theology has affirmed about freedom as the capacity for the definitive—that is, as the capacity for the eternal, the capacity to say: "forever". The priest also lives in this "forever", in this radical commitment to Christ. Christ has not gone from being a "yes" to being a "no": he has been the "Yes" and the "Amen" to all promises, a definitive yes. What does it mean to be a priest forever? Is it possible to entertain the idea of a part-time priesthood?*

A temporary priesthood has never been part of the Catholic faith. Certainly, there is a reluctance in our society to encourage young people to make an act of commitment. So young people prefer to keep their options open: they are marrying later, for example. Also in other realms of society: people change their jobs regularly; they do not want to work at the same business all the time.

So this is one place in which Christianity is clearly countercultural. And it also brings consequences for the Christian concept of marriage for life. Wedding promises are not there for as long as love lasts, but for richer and for poorer, in sickness and in health, and that parallels the promises of the priest.

7. Are there today a neo-gnosticism and a neo-Pelagianism?

Priests as preachers are called to ask themselves constantly what the faithful need on their Christian path. We see, again and again in the history of the Church, how varied are the subjects that have been emphasized. Doctrine is thus demonstrably a never-ending source of new vitality. Take, for example, the preaching of Athanasius, who insisted on the true divinity of the Son of God, consubstantial with the Father, in opposition to the challenge of Arianism, which did not understand the mystery of God; and Cyril, in his preaching, insisted on the true divine motherhood of Mary. In every age, in various ways that depended on the need, the Church has been able to show the truth and the beauty of the mystery of God, for it is only in God, and not in some supposed substitute, that man attains his fullness. We see today that Pope Francis forcefully emphasizes the danger of an old heresy: gnosticism. The Asian Fathers of the early centuries also saw a true risk in it. What is gnosticism? Is it truly a concern today? What are the signs of its rebirth?

Gnosticism was a very loose movement in the early Christian centuries, very diverse; sometimes it was very philosophical; sometimes it was influenced by the Eastern mystery religions; sometimes it was hedonistic, sometimes it was not; sometimes it was phantastic and ridiculous in its teachings; sometimes, as with the Valentinians, it was a bit more respectable. But it was very loose, like *New Age* religions: everything and nothing. It called for interest and sympathy, but not commitment. It nearly destroyed the Church.

Gnosticism comes from "gnosis", so the emphasis was on knowing things, not on doing, not on living in community. Gnosticism led to individualism and subjectivism. The gnostics also had secret traditions that were only revealed to special "elite" members. While for Christianity, it was clear that all the truths of Christianity were open to all believers when they joined the Church. For that reason we have the creed and the baptismal questions to make it quite clear that Christian doctrine is open to everybody.

All genuine religions ask their followers to make sacrifices. Christians have to take up the cross.

On the other hand, Pope Francis also speaks of the danger of Pelagianism. *It may seem as though this risk is truly a distant one for our society: I cannot imagine that a preacher like Pelagius, who was so unyielding and ascetic, would find success today and revive a religious and cultural movement based on man's moral capacities. We may be more aware today of man's limitations. But why does the pope see this danger? What relevance does it have for our postmodern world, so marked by sentimentalism and utilitarianism?*

It is certainly true that the *New Age* movement is a difficult challenge for Christianity in the West. I think the risk of Pelagianism is basically a reliance on our own strength and forces rather than relying on God. And in a modern, technological society, that is always a real danger: that we think we have the capacity to do things by ourselves without grace and redemption. Christians know that we have no "right" to heaven. I think some people are tempted to think that they have a universal human right to heaven.

We are not quietists, because we know that God has no hands but ours. The *initium fidei* comes from God: we can never "earn" our way to heaven, we will never be good enough; we are saved, not by law, but by grace. But grace enables us to act. God works through us so that we can fulfill the gospel. This was Saint Augustine's response to Pelagianism.

The Church is asked today to be capable of offering a doctrine adapted to the times. This means that what the Church preaches is not always necessarily the same: perhaps it is enough if it is substantially so, but dogma obviously evolves. I would like to add a question in that regard. Cardinal Newman not only wrote profoundly on these subjects; he himself found faith in the Catholic Church when he realized faith was not a static reality but an organic one. He realized that faith grew and developed as such. In what sense does dogma evolve? How can this perspective help us understand that Jesus' words and the faith of the Church Fathers are alive in our faith today?

Yes, the development of doctrine is essential. Jesus did not say how many books there were to be in the New Testament. The Church, with the assistance of the Holy Spirit, had to decide that. The Church had to define what Jesus meant when he spoke about God the Father, the Son, the Holy Spirit, and to arrive at the formulae of Nicaea and Constantinople.

And there are new situations today where we have to develop the tradition. In the United States today, children can be bred from selected parents with different capacities, something in the way that racehorses are bred for speed or endurance. So the Christians of the future will not tailor their children, but they will accept what God gives them;

they will generate the children by a loving act of inter-course, not in some mechanical way, and they will not abort babies because they are handicapped or deficient.

So, there is development but within the tradition.

Newman was important in this regard because for him it was clear that every new development was at the same time conservative of the tradition that went back to the *fontes*. A true development means that you do not need to dismiss any of the essentials of the tradition.

There are no backflips in the development of doctrine. It is organic. There are no ruptures in the development of doctrine and no reversals. There is massive development from an acorn to an oak. But always, it is still the DNA of the oak. That is in the acorn. And so it is with the development of doctrine. Newman wrote beautifully on that.

For example, with the invention of the pill, the doctrine of *Humanae vitae* had to deal with a lot of seriously new problems. It did so within the tradition. Or, taking now another controversial problem, we believe that the Church could never accept the possibility of homosexual marriage. That would be a reversal of our tradition.

There is also a tendency today toward a modern understanding of reality in which you shape or remake the gospel teachings according to modern understandings. That is a radical alternative. The false development, according to Newman, happens when Christianity abandons itself to a non-Christian environment. This is a development of the doctrine of modernity which swallows the Church, not a development of Christian doctrine.

Etymologically, the word "catholic" means "with respect to the whole", and it coincides in effect with the way of viewing the whole—that is, of not leaving outside it any dimension of reality.

A great theologian has said that "to see the whole in the frag-ment" is what it means to be a Catholic. Each part thus refers to a greater whole. How is it important to our lives to understand that our faith requires a global acceptance—that is, an acceptance of the whole? Can we believe only in the basic things and let some points that we consider to be "lesser" fall by the wayside? What does the history of the Church teach us about that?

It all depends on what you mean by "the whole" in that phrase you are quoting. In the English poet William Blake, we have a similar idea, but better expressed: "To see a World in a Grain of Sand / And a Heaven in a Wild Flower / Hold infinity in the palm of your hand / and Eternity in an hour". The difference between the phrase you quoted and this one is that instead of "whole", we have here "Eternity". Not just the created things, but God, who cannot be identified with the Whole, because he is transcendent; he is more than the sum of all things.

The English philosopher Anthony Flew was once seen as the world's best-known atheist. He came to a belief in God, not the personal God of Christians, through modern science, especially through the spectacular predictive power of DNA. At the macro level, the odds against the original creation, the Big Bang, developing into human thinking life on our tiny planet are almost impossible to imagine; one chance in trillions of trillions.

It is a further step to acknowledge that the Supreme Intelligence or Architect is also good, loving, and interested in us. One vital task of the priest is to help others take this step.

III

THE PRIEST AS PHYSICIAN AND HEALER OF WOUNDS

*A Conversation with Monsignor Livio Melina,
Holder of the Chair in Moral Theology
at the Pontifical John Paul II Institute
for Studies on Marriage and Family at
the Catholic University of America*

1. The vocation: Discovering a great life

*Don Livio, when you reflect on all your years in the priesthood,
what do you see? What have been the greatest gifts in your life as
a priest? What have been the most serious difficulties? I imagine
that after more than thirty-five years in the priesthood, one looks
back on a steady flow of promises and fruitfulness. What aspects
of it can you share with us? In what ways has your ministry
borne fruit?*

You are posing a difficult question, because I do not feel
capable of weighing up so many years of experience and
priestly life: I do not even know if it is appropriate. I feel
something similar to Saint Paul's reluctance to judge his
own life. What I see more and more clearly in these years
of priesthood is that there is an incalculable disproportion

between the greatness of the gift that has been given me, which I find endlessly astonishing, and my frailty, my weakness, my inadequacy.

But, above all, looking at my life as a priest, I feel gratitude for what I have undeservedly seen flourish around me. Especially in those I have had the privilege of teaching, because I have devoted a great part of my priestly ministry to that. My priesthood has been dedicated to serving the truth. First, in the Congregation for the Doctrine of the Faith and, then, teaching at the Pontifical John Paul II Institute for Studies on Marriage and Family.

It is true that I have never left off being directly engaged in pastoral work, as a participant in the life of a Roman parish for more than twenty years and, over these last few years, in preaching, celebrating the Eucharist, and hearing confessions in the Basilica of Saint John Lateran. At the same time, from the very beginning of my priesthood, I have been able to live a pastoral ministry with the families I have accompanied.

But the main, dominant part of my ministry has been to serve the truth through study and teaching. And I have seen a great fruitfulness thanks to that, and also because I have recognized that the truth that has been entrusted to me is not a truth of books or doctrines but, first and foremost, a personal truth: a personal truth that is Christ, who is the truth in person and who seeks out individual persons to foster greatness in their lives.

I therefore see that, beyond great personalities, my life has been particularly marked by the priestly friendships with which I have been able to live the ministry entrusted to me. First, in living with a group of priests to whom I am very grateful because they have allowed me to deepen my devotion to the Lord and live it with them. Then again, in the Congregation for the Doctrine of the Faith, in the team that came together to work there. And later the friendship with my colleagues as professors, especially in the Pontifical John Paul II Institute. These relationships have become for me the locus of confirmation, of encounter, and of support in the daily development of my ministry.

I could say, in von Balthasar's words, that God's presence in my life as a priest has been constant in accordance with the Lord's method—that is, of latency and guidance, or, as Balthasar says, *Latenz* and *Begleitung*. This means that the Lord conceals himself out of respect for my freedom ("latency"), but at the same time he acts as my guide, so as not to let me stray too far off course. I have been able to experience this many times. I am very grateful for this form of discreet but continuous presence of God in my life.

Who are the priests who have had the most direct and deepest influence on your life? I do not mean just priests from your childhood or youth or at the time of your vocation, but also priests whom you have encountered during your ministry, your teachers in the art of priestly life, your guides on the paths of your ministry. Why have these priests had such a strong influence? And also, what books have been truly illuminating companions to you?

It is always hard to be specific. There are direct and evident influences in life. There are other influences that are more veiled, but maybe more potent, in the communion of saints. One figure I remember, for example, is the priest who baptized me. He was a village parish priest, but he was very attentive to social and cultural problems: he truly taught my father life, and he was a good companion to me in my first steps along the vocational path right after primary school, during my adolescence.

The experience that most clearly fostered my priestly vocation came in the movement of Communion and Liberation: there I discovered, with true joy, the consonance between faith and life. That is, God's closeness to life and his capacity for renewing it, for giving it meaning, with a freshness that for me has been truly the fragrance of God in my life. In this context, I see close at hand the figure of Don Romano Vescovi, from Reggio Emilia, who is the one who always accompanied me and in whose person I began to see the possibility of a fruitful priesthood, full of joy and also of fruitfulness for others. But I also benefited from the great influence and great enlightenment, and also the personal acquaintance, of the Servant of God Don Luigi Giussani, the founder and inspiration of the Communion and Liberation movement. It was in that environment that the possibility of the priesthood germinated in me.

I should add that, within Communion and Liberation, I also was blessed by a very exceptional spiritual friendship with now-Cardinal Scola. That friendship was reinforced in everyday life, together with other priests, during my first years in Rome, and it continued in the form of a truly singular spiritual fatherhood. Don Angelo had a gift for companionship, always there with a close camaraderie and ready helping hand as I made my way forward, and he was able to strengthen me with his embrace in the most difficult and trying moments on my priestly path. It was with him that I learned to understand the fruitfulness of my priesthood. But perhaps his conversation and witness helped me most by contributing to my discovery of the great correlation between my humanity and the mission to which I had been called.

In this context, I give endless thanks to the Lord for the two great touchstones with which I was blessed during my years working in Rome—first and foremost, Cardinal Ratzinger, in his daily life in the Congregation for the Doctrine of the Faith. He was a teacher of theology who accompanied me in my intellectual maturation, but he also bore witness to that humility and Christian humanism which is capable of opening itself in wonder to the gift of Christ's presence and then attesting to it in priestly life.

Secondly, there is the great figure of Saint John Paul II, whose capacity for listening and mystical depth, as well as his gift of his whole self to the mission and priestly celibacy, I was able to experience in personal acquaintance. In my encounters with him, he showed a cordial fatherliness and attention to the individuality of each person.

All this was a great help to me. Certainly there were moments of trial and tribulation. I would say that this is a moment of particular trial in my life. But I have always been convinced, and am now, that it is precisely in these moments of trial that God prepares a new fruitfulness: unseen, a new fruitfulness is gestating.

You asked, too, about what books have been especially fruitful for me. It is hard to choose the ones that have been most significant or pivotal, but there are great texts, poetic and mystical in nature rather than immediately theological, that have helped me. For example, Charles Péguy has been a crucial point of reference, in his poetic works and in the witness he bears in his plays. I have also felt very close to T. S. Eliot as well as to the great Christian literature of France, from Mauriac to Bernanos and Léon Bloy; the witness of Giovanni Papini regarding his conversion helped me a great deal when I was young; Chesterton has always been a companion. And later, to mention the theologians, I found one book particularly crucial: Jean LeClercq's work *The Love of Learning and the Desire for God*, which is a testament, through the experience of medieval monastic theology, to Christianity's capacity for searching out the heart of man.

Among the great theologians, one renowned point of reference that is beloved and always reread is the theology of Ratzinger, as well as that of Newman, de Lubac, Balthasar, the exegete Schlier, and later also an Italian theologian who has accompanied me, and still does today, with both theological and spiritual writings: Giacomo Cardinal Biffi.

Don Livio, you were an adolescent in the years of the sexual revolution, which from 1968 on has spread throughout Western society and also in the Church. These were the years following the council, as well as the years of divorce and abortion laws, when it seemed as though an earthquake were shaking the foundations under our feet and we had to reach out for support. You saw your vocation during those years; where did the light you saw come from, and how was this light able to illuminate other dimensions of life as well?

Yes, those were the times of the sexual revolution. But that was not all. This revolution was part of a more profound change in our guiding principles. It was a moment in which tradition as such was being called into question. There was a desire for a rupture with the world of the past, in search of a new authenticity, but also with ideological inflections that have since manifested themselves in all their destructive force.

My discovery of Communion and Liberation was critical for me. A book occasioned this discovery, because it bore witness to life in a community and thus became the vehicle for a living and vital encounter with that community. This book was titled *Oltre la contestazione* [Beyond dispute], a title that is itself very significant. What did my encounter with Communion and Liberation in this context mean for me? It was an invitation to take seriously my desire, my questioning, and the question of renewal that stirred the younger generations of the time. It was about looking at human nature with sympathy, but also about recognizing that the Church offers a humanity, offers a truth in following Christ that is of the highest order and can value this human desire without censure; and that the path, therefore, does not lead through a rupture with the past but rather through the experience today of the newness of Christianity as the fulfillment of all that is human. This witness again offered me the face of the Church as Mother and, in that motherhood, the renewed desire to accept what Christianity offers.

The Church has revealed herself to me as the living presence in which Christ is alive and present; as a community in which what Christianity offers is still current, not a relic of the past; and at the same time as the validation of a past that opens up our perspective on the future—that is, the presence of the Church as a response to man's desire.

In your life as a priest, what has been your experience of the priest's fatherhood? How have you lived it in your ministry? What were the moments in which you were able to see most clearly that a priest is a father?

I should answer first with something that has stayed with me since the day of my ordination, engraved in my memory and in my heart. It was something that my father said to me: "How thrilling: now you, who are my son, have become my father!" This sentence has been lodged in my heart ever since. The priestly fatherhood that I have known is a fatherhood that is realized by leaving space for the fatherhood of God. It is a little like Saint Joseph's fatherhood, and it is in the school of Saint Joseph that I try to live it. It is therefore conditioned on the virginity of the relationship with the other person, what Don Giussani called "possession at a distance". This means the affective intensity of a participation in the life of the other person, in his questions, in his searches, in his suffering, on his rocky path, and also in his joys and enthusiasms; but it is a participation in trusting the Holy Spirit, the Other who alone can answer the questions a person carries in his heart. All fruitfulness derives from the Holy Spirit.

I see this "possession at a distance" as being realized above all in the sacrament of confession, in the embrace of this sacrament, through which the priest's word, at least as I experience it as confessor and as I try to experience it when I myself am confessing and reconciling myself with God, is a discreet word that must leave space for the witness of the Other's Word. In spiritual counseling, this certainly becomes real in a different form, because the spiritual accompaniment of others involves entering more directly into their questions and requests for clarification, help, and correction, whereas the key element of the sacrament of confession is the objectivity of the gift of grace that the Lord entrusts to the priest. The priest's discretion as the medium of reconciliation with God through the Church is more in evidence in confession. There this form of priestly fatherhood is recognized in a very particular way.

You began to study moral theology shortly after being ordained as a priest. These were years of a great many new initiatives, and I suppose it could not have been easy for you to find a productive path forward. How did you understand what was at stake during those years? Who were your teachers?

Especially throughout my seminary studies and later in earning my degree in moral theology, I was living the years of confusion that followed *Humanae vitae* and that precipitated discussion of the very foundations of the Church's moral doctrine. Though I sought and found professors of high intellectual stature and also great spiritual profundity, what prevailed was confusion and a deaf resistance to the traditional morality proposed by the Church. No doubt this line of thinking was an attempt to rise above a casuistic morality, but that attempt fell afoul of an even more insidious danger: the subjectivization of conscience. I never found that point of view convincing, and I spent those years in search of a new alternative.

I found that alternative in one of my professors during those years: the now-Cardinal Caffarra. The decisive factor in my acquaintance with Professor Caffarra was his insistence that a moral life had to be the expression of a truth, of a truth about the good, of a foundation that was not just a subjectivist or casuistic response to the moral question but that, rather, had a true foundation. I always recall, with emotion and gratitude, Cardinal Caffarra's lessons in Bologna on Christ as the center of morality. Christ, he would tell us, is the truth about the good, the revelation of the truth regarding the good in man. This teaching was being developed during those years by the great Saint John Paul II.

Along with this there was a second decisive element in which I could immerse myself in my doctoral thesis. I am referring to the thinking of Saint Thomas Aquinas. With a group of students at the Pontifical Gregorian University, among whom a great friendship had been born in the

shared adventure of seeking new paths and better responses
in the face of dissatisfaction with a certain type of teaching, we set out together in search of a new point of view
on these questions in our study of Saint Thomas Aquinas.
What fascinated us was not simply his familiar theology
of the law or his reflections on conscience, but rather the
general rediscovery of perspective on the virtues, on their
role along the path of man's happiness, with all their influence on energizing the human endeavor. With the virtues,
we reevaluated the passions, the desires, the history of each
individual, offering a new principle for the unification
of conduct that promoted a better integration of the law
and conscience. This fresh rediscovery of Saint Thomas
was critical for me.

2. What light can we offer the priest in the "liquid" society?

*The problems you are describing, however, are different from the
problems that a priest faces today. I understand that today,
too, we are living through an earthquake, which Benedict XVI
described as a relativism that threatens the very foundations on
which the lives of so many priests are built. The late-modern
crisis has invaded the Church, as well, with a very worrisome
relativism. It is the sort of relativism that sees faith as something
incomplete, an evolving idea that is always being reformulated and
never is definitive. What is more, the word "truth" has practically
disappeared from ecclesial language. A priest would be best served
by not looking for certitude in faith, because that would make
him rigid in the face of the various shapes of reality and people;
better, perhaps, to seek assurance in being a "searcher". In his
first encyclical, however, Pope Francis insists on faith as a light
that can illuminate a person's entire existence, precisely because it*

is born of love. How can today's priest address this profound and novel crisis of late modernity?

I do not believe today's problems are that different from those that I found when I began my study of moral theology. It may be that there has today been a sharpening of a difficulty that has been with the Church since the beginning of the modern era and is expressed in many forms, especially in moral theology. Certainly, moral theology became the most visible and obvious locale of what Paul VI defined as the great challenge that Christianity had to come to grips with—that is, the separation between faith and life. But this separation should be seen as more than a difficulty of coherence or authenticity. The problem of coherence appears in every era; it is an ever-present problem. But the current difficulty affects more than coherence, touching on the conception of life that does not take faith as its point of departure, that thinks of faith as an abstraction, in such a way that it takes points of reference that differ from those that faith proposes. For that reason, the great body of thought of Saint John Paul II and Benedict XVI has pointed to a path that is still current as a response to this problem, to this separation, and that consists of recovering faith as a light on the truth of the good that gives meaning to life.

The first great encyclical of Pope Francis, *Lumen fidei*, has reaffirmed this path. This encyclical has unfortunately been neglected, ignored even by theological studies and not studied in depth. In it, he shows the unity of faith and love, the personalized character of faith, and how faith is at the root of renewal, how it enters into a life and renews it.

I see the term "truth" as critically important in this context. But it refers to a truth that is born of a personal encounter and is therefore a light and not a formula, which

is just what this great encyclical says. A light that illuminates the greatness of all that is human.

I believe it is precisely this point that can help us understand the great danger of our late-modern era, which is
the danger of nihilism, with its banalization of the human.
We are offered a dual form of nihilism that culminates,
regrettably, in the violence in our cities that has become
a day-to-day anxiety for all of us. On the one hand, there
is the nihilism of a presumed faith that rejects reason. On
the other, there is the nihilism of a reason that rejects faith
and ends up denying its very capacity for the truth—the
nihilism of an Islamist fundamentalism and the nihilism of
Western relativism. To address this double nihilism, it is
important to defend the rationality of faith and the openness of reason to faith. A faith that is the friend of reason,
and a reason that is the friend of faith, as Pope Benedict XVI saw the matter. The fruitfulness of the approach
taken by Francis in his first encyclical lies in love being
what makes it possible for faith and reason to meet. Of
course, that love is not just a feeling but an event, a gift
that we receive and that transforms us. Juan José Pérez-
Soba's studies have highlighted this aspect. Advancing
along this path and offering a great vision of love and its
truth is the great challenge to be met in order to overcome the separation between faith and life that is the great
drama of our time.

*I understand that I am speaking to a moral theologian. But it is
true that today morality has a "bad name". It appears that being
a "moralist" is even a sin. The priest even fears being labeled as
such, believes that, rather than raising moral issues, which are
always thorny, it is better to try to help people in other parts of
their lives. But what is morality, really? Does it not have to do*

precisely with a life's greatness and beauty? And might it not therefore be central to the ministry of the priest?

The bad name of morality, as has been said very accurately, has its origin in an underdeveloped idea of what morality is, in a "moralist" idea of morality, which is separate precisely from the desire that guides life, the essential desire of fulfillment, of happiness, and thus sets aside the great spiritual goals that give light to life in order to concentrate on conforming to a formal law. So conceived, morality becomes something oppressive and limited, an attempt to control acts with norms. Freedom rebels against this: it does not accept being limited by senseless norms.

A certain Protestant theology has reacted against this moralistic idea, setting "preaching" (*kerygma*) against "teaching" (*didachē*) in morality. And it has attempted to rescue Christianity from moralistic or puritanical reduction through the rediscovery of a *kerygma* separated from morality. But doing so has gutted preaching, because it has thereby been made irrelevant: it does not speak to human desires in all their variety and greatness.

Christianity, in contrast, is the proclamation of a new life; and, in this sense, the first form of it, its earliest name, is "way" (see Jn 14:6). It is a path on which Christ's dominion over life and his capacity to transform it are manifested. Christianity is an event of love that is given and, in being given and requiring a response from man, communicates a new life and makes it possible to live it.

How does Christianity offer a path? By offering happiness as a goal for the present: "the kingdom of God has come upon you" (Mt 12:28). Anyone who recognizes the gift he has received understands what it means for his freedom—that is, for his deeds: in them the fate of his persona, of his identity, is at stake, as we understand in the contribution that Professor Grygiel has made. In this sense, it is necessary to rediscover the profound unity between the person and his deeds. "Thus you will know them by their fruits" (Mt 7:20). It is through his deeds that a person is brought to fruition, attains fulfillment, matures in history. Deeds are not merely external actions that alter the state of things in the world. Through his deeds, a person generates and regenerates himself and fulfills his life: but he can also lose himself, when his deeds contradict his truth, his desire, his ultimate end. The profound unity of person and deed is therefore a first decisive point at which to enter the human drama.

And together with this, the Christian proposition is a proclamation that is transformed into life. That is how to overcome the opposition referred to before—in Dodd's theology, for example—between *kerygma* and *didachē*. And this unity is found in the very preaching and the very teachings of the early Church. McDonald, another Anglican scholar of the Bible, has shown the reciprocal connection and correspondence between *kerygma* and *didachē*, between proclamation and moral teaching.

What is at stake in moral life, then, is not the jejune correspondence of conduct with the law but, rather, the path of man's fulfillment: this is the fulfillment that God wants to give to man.

3. What is happiness? A beautiful ideal?

Allow me now to ask you about a sweeping subject: What is the relationship between morality and happiness? It seems that today no one talks anymore about that source of enthusiasm in life: happiness. It seems as though this expansive word that the great philosophers and Jesus himself used so forcefully has turned into a banality or, even worse, is used today only in the context of marketing. *Do we still need to use this word?*

It is the crucial word in classic morality: the word "happiness". All the great philosophers and theologians who have spoken of morality, from Aristotle through Augustine to Thomas Aquinas, have seen happiness as the great horizon in which the moral life of man finds meaning. Pinckaers' studies in this respect are very enlightening. But modernity, as we know, has cast doubt on this link. This is especially true of Kant, who thought of morality as being at odds with happiness; the search for happiness would render man's acts self-interested and subjective, and they would then not be moral.

We often have an outdated idea of happiness. We think of it as being a function of our mood, not a result of our deeds: happiness would be the feeling of satisfaction that seizes us when our desires are met. This is an emotivist idea of happiness: it is not the vision of the great Christian philosophical tradition, in which happiness was not a state but rather a fullness of action, of life, of excellence. Anyone who wants to understand this perspective need simply pick up the Lord's first sermon: the Beatitudes.

The Beatitudes are Jesus' great homily in which he lays out his moral position. The Beatitudes reveal Jesus' conception of happiness. Jesus unquestionably proposes happiness. I remember the image, the beautiful image, that Mauriac presents in his *Life of Jesus*, in which he imagines what happened there. The people surrounding Jesus heard his words, heard these eight great promises. But those who were farthest from him did not hear the words very clearly; some of those words may have been lost, wafted away in the mountain air. In any case, there was at least one word that they heard continuously and understood, that word repeated over and over again in the echo of that mountain: "Blessed ... blessed ... blessed". And they understood that they were there because of the promise of happiness that Jesus, with his word and his person, represented for each of them.

The Beatitudes, especially since the time of Saint Augustine's commentary but also of many other patristic commentaries, express the deep unity between morality and happiness—a deep unity that is, however, paradoxical, in the sense that the happiness Jesus promises is not apparent, does not answer to the canons of happiness that man can understand in his everyday life. It is a hidden happiness that is realized in tears, in poverty, and in the suffering of injustice. But, above all, it is the blessing that secretly allows us to participate in the life of Christ. This is the secret of happiness: in day-to-day life there is a way of living, which is to say of acting, that in the paradox that it comprises permits us, however, to follow Jesus, to unite ourselves with him. The secret of happiness is following Christ, conforming with him in a way that Christ proposes to his people, and that means sharing in suffering, in persecution—and thereby experiencing a foretaste of the joy that Jesus lives through his intimacy with the Father.

Christian conduct joins us with God. It is therefore joyous, fulfilling conduct. Yes, still in a paradoxical way. For that reason, in what is hidden and in the cross, there is a foretaste of our resurrection. The paradox of happiness lies in its being found when it is not sought; that is, when one renounces happiness in the form of satisfaction and follows Christ, he finds the fullness of the Father. The soul itself is saved when life is lost, when it is prepared to be lost; it is attained when it is given. In this sense, happiness is the great subject matter of morality. But it is an element that is illuminated only in the light of love, in the light of recognition of the gift that a person has been given and the light of love's generous answer that, when it is acted on, paradoxically reveals that that is where God is.

To forget this word is to renounce the greatness of man: because man is called to something greater than himself, to union with God. But to say it without clarification is to foster a poor understanding of Christianity.

When we speak of happiness—that is, of fullness, of fulfillment—do we not risk speaking of an "ideal"? You would be speaking to me of what "should be", which does not match, however, the reality of our life, so fragile and subject to so many influences. Might not this presentation of happiness as an "ideal" perhaps be a great danger for preaching the gospel? Jesus would thus be reduced to a great preacher or even a great moralist. This was precisely the idea that a fourth-century ascetic had: Pelagius. According to him, Jesus was the great exemplar, and his words were the great spur prompting us to overcome our sloth. According to Pelagius, this is what we would receive from the Son of God. But where is there grace in this? What is the relationship between grace and the path of man, his fate, his happiness? Does grace point the way to and along the path? How?

Yes, sometimes the Beatitudes have also been interpreted as simple ideals, as a moral ideal that is very high, it is true, but also hard to attain. Perhaps these great spiritual currents, these great temptations, accompany the history of the Church, assuming different shapes but with a common substance that connects them. In any case, these imposing words, like "Pelagianism", can sometimes become clichés, slogans that are repeated and used as catapults, as weapons with which to demonize adversaries. Pelagianism, however, corresponds to an enduring temptation of

Christianity, a radical alternative, because it reduces Christianity to an ideal and puts the entire burden of realizing it on human capabilities; it reduces Christianity to a program to be carried out. And this is certainly a temptation for morality, because it gives primacy to morality, posits morality as the essential element of Christianity, its key. That would reduce Christianity to morality, to a program that we must carry out by engaging our own strength.

This would certainly support rigorism, which is the claim of an answer that goes beyond what is humanly possible. But it also could lead to permissivism, acquiescence in our own fragility as we confront the impossibility of attaining such a high ideal. The overtones of this today are very symptomatic: anyone who sees Christian preaching as an ideal that is very difficult to attain will end up adapting the ideal to his own capabilities—that is, will take his judgment of his capabilities as the criterion by which to judge his conscience. Or, what amounts to the same thing, he will reduce the way he judges his conscience to the level of what he judges to be his capacity. And he thereby loses the good news of Christian morality as the synergy between freedom and divine grace.

It is against this temptation that the encyclical *Veritatis splendor* put us on our guard. It says that man cannot measure his true potential by simply looking at his frail and sinful nature and that his true potential is what he perceives it to be in grace. It is grace that gives the measure of man's true potential.

What, then, is moral theology? We can say that moral theology is the study of this synergy between the gift of grace and human freedom; the gift always comes first and is always greater, because what is offered is first of all the gift of healing and the gift of a perspective that goes beyond what humans can foresee. But it is precisely because grace is so great that it not only does not exclude man's reply but includes it. Morality is not the first word in Christian life. It is a reply to a gift received, and it therefore is secondary. But only in that reply is beauty expressed, because it is an expression of the symphony of God with man: what God's art is capable of doing in us, what human freedom generated by grace is capable of. Morality is a word that, between the gift of grace and its fulfillment, becomes necessary. We are justified by faith, but we will be judged by our works. Our works are necessarily included as a mediation between the beginning that God opens in our life and the promise with which he wants to fulfill us, relying on our reply.

I agree that grace thus appears as a new beginning that points the way to our fate. But, all the same, it seems to me that the temptation of today's priest is precisely that of presenting a grace that does indeed herald our destiny and does open an inner path, but that does not change life on the exterior, neither in our relationships nor in our desires. It is thus a matter of a "spiritual grace". It is something different from Pelagianism: we find ourselves today confronting a rebirth of gnosticism. Is that so?

Some writers decry precisely this characteristic of our time. It is a little paradoxical because gnosticism is characterized by a valuation of knowledge over faith and by a spiritualization of faith over corporeality. And yet our time seems to value the corporeal highly and greatly devalue the spiritual. But these forms of paradoxical temptations are a fixture of the history of the Church, although their name and symbolism change, sometimes being turned on their head. This new gnosticism is a gnosticism in which the separation between spirit and

flesh, underneath the apparent valorization of the corporeal, nevertheless confirms the deprecation of the flesh,
or of history and everything in history that is concrete
and comes to us through symbols.

I would say that the current temptation is that of thinking of grace in fleshless form—that is, thinking of grace
apart from the economy of the Incarnation, apart from
the economy of the Church, apart from the economy of the
sacraments. This is thinking of an economy of the spirit
that dispenses with the flesh or acts in the spirit beyond the
objective situations in which the individual and humanity
itself find themselves. Henri de Lubac spoke of a spiritual
posterity of Joachim de Flore. It is the constant temptation to think that everything is headed toward "golden
years", after those of the Father and of the Son, an "age
of the Spirit" in which salvation is achieved without the
sacraments, without the commandments, without institutions, with a logic and frame of mind that goes beyond
reason—that is, with a kind of knowledge or *gnosis* of
the spirit that is not attained in accordance with reason, the
sacraments, the institution, the commandments: a charity
without morality, without commandments, a charity that
can dispense with the commandments and the virtues.
And, furthermore, it would involve a Spirit that could act
against reason. The Spirit is certainly greater than human
reason and can therefore point to new paths; but he never
can or wants to go beyond Christ, who is the *Logos*. The
Spirit can act beyond the institution and sacraments of
the Church, but he is always the Spirit of Christ who
operates with a view to the edification of the Church and,
therefore, in accordance with Scholastic theology, always
operates with a view to the sacraments, to build the visible
and sacramental reality of the Church. That is how Christ's
Spirit is capable of regenerating the Father's original plan,

making it possible for everything to participate in the *Logos* in which it was created.

Yes, you are right, gnosticism is precisely a great temptation of late modernity, because it has forgotten the Creator and the *logos* (or meaning) of his work.

4. Do the sacraments transform our being, energize our freedom?

These reflections allow me to ask you also about the form in which the Christian receives grace. It comes about in a sacramental way: in those humble signs made by the priest there is a unique grandeur, a divine action. How do these sacraments act in our lives? Do they truly transform us? What do they transform? What relationship is there between Christ's action in the sacraments and God's action in the origin of creation? I am trying to get at the great question of how the sacraments regenerate the Father's plan after man has destroyed it. Today, however, in the life of so many postmodern Christians, the sacraments are instead the opportunity to have a religious experience, but not a regeneration of one's being and corporeal relationships.

What is at stake in the sacraments is the unsurpassable truth of the Incarnation and the means that derive from it. Christ saves the flesh through the flesh. He saves the tangible flesh of man, his body, his relationships, his history. From flesh to flesh: here is the logic of the sacraments that José Granados' studies have thrown into relief. This is the place where salvation happens. Saint Thomas Aquinas, when he speaks of the new law, precisely in order to overcome Joachim de Flore's difficulty of an age of the Spirit that dispenses with the Church, sets out the subject of the Incarnation as the great argument that identifies the nature of the new law and frees it from the errors of an excessive spiritualization.

The sacrament is not, however, the satisfaction of an inner need for spirituality. This is often one of the dangers we face. The danger consists of the reduction of the Christian experience to a vague religiosity, in which the primacy of the subjective conscience leads each of us to take from Christianity what he wants, what he likes the most, what he finds most convenient, according to an intimist logic of religion that reduces it to individual experience. We need to rediscover the great reality of the encounter with Christ that touches a person and, in touching his life, changes him. Unfortunately, when the Church is not experienced as a specific body that generates a new life and forms a new mentality, Christianity remains exposed to this fatal danger that is the dissolution of its profound nature.

On the other hand, neither is it sufficient simply to propose again the *ex opere operato* of the Council of Trent. It is true that every sacrament has its own strength and efficacy. But it enters into human life and regenerates freedom and, therefore, the relationships in which we live. Today, perhaps more than ever, we seemingly need to see how the sacramental grace particular to each sacrament is capable of regenerating specific dimensions of the Father's original plan, motivating us to live our relationships in harmony with that plan. The Church of the Fathers was able to do this work with true creativity by developing the mystagogical catechisms, in which they showed how the sacrament caused a person to flower and accompanied this flowering with specific practices.

I am in complete agreement that the sacraments transform us. But we come across so many people today who, despite their feelings, live in a manner that is contrary to the gospel: I am talking about people who are slaves to the world of drugs or sexuality or work; slaves by their own choice, who end up finding themselves in situations that are objectively contrary to Jesus' words, but who want even so to believe and come to him. We talk today about the importance of initiating processes, opening paths to people, and meeting them on their own ground. My question is aimed at understanding if something has changed in the Catholic way of thinking: the theology I studied distinguished between death and life, between the path on which to accompany a person who has not entered divine life and the path on which to accompany a person who has. The need for conversion—that is, a change in the person's way of life—used to lie between these two. But it seems today that conversion has become more of a change in feelings than a change in behavior. Great theology understood that, for anyone who had converted and accepted grace, there was a path, but the path was called "progress of charity". On the other hand, anyone who lacked charity was asked to convert. What is the difference between a process and progress? What is conversion? How does it appear in our lives? How does the grace of God energize our freedom so that we can convert?

The Lord certainly comes to me where I am; he is the Good Shepherd who seeks the lost sheep where it is, among the most dangerous pitfalls, there where the sheep has gone to lose its life. The Church and the priest are called to search for individuals where they are, where they have been lost and hidden. It seems to me that this is the great pastoral invitation of Pope Francis: Reach out to all; show them that the Lord makes haste to seek out everyone and make it possible for them to find him; show them that for everyone there is an open path in the actual life of the Church, that there is no place so far away that Christ cannot reach it and no path on which there is a point of no return.

And yet there is a particular logic to this path of return: it is a path of conversion, and it implies a specific moment, that of rejecting evil and returning to the good. And this is a decisive moment, because between an existence in sin and a life in charity there is a qualitative difference that cannot be suppressed or disguised. There is a qualitative difference between good and evil; a radical choice must be made between, on the one hand, a life of sin, a life enclosed in one's own selfishness, and, on the other hand, a life open to God and open to others, in love. It is the moment of radical conversion, followed by the period of progress in the good. There is a moment of repudiating evil and a period in which, once the path of the good has been chosen, one must walk step by step toward the consolidation of the good, toward a greater generosity and a deeper and more intimate adherence to the good.

But conversion can also be prepared for. I think it is important to emphasize this. It is certainly the case that it is up to the priest to await the conversion of a person, but not just await it passively; await it, instead, as the Latin term *tendere* says, by reaching out to it, preparing it.

There are sacraments that strongly imply this change, above all the sacrament of baptism, which is the sacrament of conversion. And it becomes real for us in the sacrament of reconciliation. This sacrament is a form of new baptism in which a fallen Christian, even one who has fallen far, can return and be renewed in the grace of baptism. Conversion certainly is above all liberation from selfish love, to enable the convert to love God and live a life oriented toward him. In the stubbornness of sin, one is oriented toward oneself in everything. God breaks that intransigence and breaks into one's life with a new love: he opens a new beginning for freedom, as the studies of Stephan Kampowski have shown. His love corrects our deformed love of ourselves, which exploits everything for one's own account, transforming it into self-love. In that regard, it is worth recalling the celebrated and important words of Bernanos' *Diary of a Country Priest*. He says there: "Grace is to forget oneself. But if all pride was dead in us, the grace of all graces would be to love oneself humbly, as one would love any of the suffering members of Jesus Christ."

The difference between death and life that you are talking about should be understood, then, as the difference between the death of a relationship (with God and the Other) and life in a relationship (with God and others); and it is not a matter of emotion felt in a moment but, rather, of a stable resolve in the relationship. It is a difference that puts one's freedom at risk, the heart that may or may not be united with the loved one. Anyone who has lost this life in a relationship with God because of a serious sin cannot recover it by himself: it requires the action of Christ, who with his Spirit regenerates his heart. The path to this regeneration is the path of conversion, which sometimes involves a long process and requires the priest to know how to accompany it, awakening the desire for God and the recognition and rejection of what has broken that relationship. It is not always easy, because our desires get in the way of our seeing the truth about our actions. Progress, on the contrary, involves the growth of the gift already received. Saint Thomas saw that charity could grow in us, could mature, because it is a friendship, and that is how he spoke of the progress of charity. Process prepares and clears the path, but it still does not regenerate: progress gives us wings and enables us to fly. If we mix the *therapy of the conversion process* with strategies specific to the *progress of charity*, we will make it more difficult for the first therapy to attain its goal, which is for the person to

abandon sin and come out of himself to embrace friendship with God. Because he will not clearly understand the
moment in which he finds himself and the steps he needs
to take.

*I understand that our liberty is injured and so is our desire, as our
relationships are also injured. The origin of the injury is deeper
than our choices and also than our life. It is rooted in the absolute
beginning, in the sinfulness of our first mother and father and their
decision to defy God: we have all been affected by their sin. From
that time on, we have seen God as a stranger, and his law, which
is also foreign to us, has been turned into a yoke, into a nightmare
from which to free ourselves. How has Christ overcome this wound
to our being and our desire?*

This wound is certainly deep in the relationship with
God; it is a wound that, from that relationship, has gone
on to be transmitted to other relationships. I think it could
be defined as "doubt about original love". The wound is
the rupture between the Creator and the creature, a creature who doubts the foundation of life itself, doubts that
it had its origin in a love. And so desire becomes anxious,
indistinct, and indefinite. Desire is nostalgia for the great, for
the stars, as its very etymology shows (*de-siderium* in Latin,
sidera = stars), a nostalgia for God: having lost his orientation
toward God, man vacillates anxiously among things.

How does our encounter with the Lord Jesus heal us?
It heals us precisely by showing us love as the foundation
and, furthermore, giving us anew the love of God as the
foundation of our life—that is, giving us his Spirit. And so
desire is healed. Because desire is not the first word. Desire
is preceded by a love, and, because it is preceded by a love,
it becomes hope.

Christ the physician. What does this title that Augustine gives Christ mean to you? Could one also speak of the priest as a physician? What does the priest heal?

First of all, the subject of Christ as physician is a great theme of the Gospels. Jesus presents himself as a physician. "Those who are well have no need of a physician, but those who are sick; I came not to call the righteous, but sinners" (Mk 2:17); "he went about doing good and healing all that were oppressed by the devil" (Acts 10:38). But he wanted to show us in his healings that he was a physician for a deeper wound: " 'But that you may know that the Son of man has authority on earth to forgive sins'—he said to the man who was paralyzed—'I say to you, rise, take up your bed and go home'" (Lk 5:24). Christ seeks out sinners. He presents his life, his mission, as the mission of a physician who heals the wound of sin.

Beyond the Gospels, the image of Christ as physician is very beloved and very present among the Church Fathers: with this image, they wanted to express the way Jesus heals us. He heals us with his wounds. It is a cure through the gift of himself and through the fact of his having taken our wounds upon himself. In the second of the *Four Quartets*, the Anglo-American writer T. S. Eliot speaks of the "wounded surgeon", who cures us precisely through his own wounds; he excises the tumor of sin from us by taking it upon himself.

And who is the priest? The priest, we could say, is not the physician; he is the physician's assistant; we could say he is the nurse. Eliot himself defines the Church as the "dying nurse", who, while she is participating in the healing, offers herself and shares in the salvational sacrifice. The priest is he who leads to the physician, because only the physician can cure and heal. But to do so, the priest has to assume the special viewpoint of Jesus, who in his mercy is able to understand the tragedy in which man finds himself: that tragedy is not that he cannot satisfy his whims but, rather, that he cannot bring his life to fruition as a great and beautiful life. But because Jesus is a physician, he knows where the root of this tragedy lies: in sin, which separates man from God. He knows the real tragedy, beyond the apparent good fortune in which the sinner lives, which is to lose the greatness and nobility of the human, rejecting God in favor of some substitute. But, in addition, he knows the risk that this life carries with it: of losing eternal life forever. The priest as assistant to Christ the physician shares this deep vision, this deep compassion that is born of seeing the truth about man's sin and the great danger that man will lose himself if he persists in a life of sin.

5. Why is the dedication of the Good Samaritan the path to follow?

In the history of theology, the Good Samaritan has been identified with Christ. It is precisely the Good Samaritan who may be able to act as a model for the priest and his ministry. The compassion of which this part of the Gospel speaks to us has led the Samaritan to apply a series of remedies to the wounded man's body. It is true that these remedies constitute an "invasive" act upon the wounded man's body, a crucial act, which touches the wounded flesh and enters the tendons and tissues of the man. Might it not be necessary today for the priest, as well, to be "invasive" in this way? Or is it not the reverse: Would it not be better for the priest to act less exigently, not to ask so much from the poor invalid, not to ask him to make almost inhuman efforts by opening his wounds and requiring him to get to his feet with the Samaritan?

The great tradition of Western wisdom reminds us that a merciful physician is one who is not afraid to inflict pain if need be. A physician who does not apply a painful remedy when faced with a serious illness confuses compassion with mercy: he will never be able to heal. It is necessary for a pastor to be courageous and realistic. The art of being a pastor is an art of love that requires realism and decisiveness: the realism to call a spade a spade. A cancer can certainly not be cured by saying it is a cold, or that, yes, there is a cancer, but the patient's body still has many healthy parts. Suffice it to recall that Saint Gregory the Great, in his *Regla pastoral*, especially castigated pastors who, to curry favor with their flock and make themselves popular, kept silence regarding the seriousness of sins.

Realism is necessary for seeing the seriousness of evil, as *decisiveness* is necessary for intervening with the intention of liberating the flock from it. Without this courage of the truth, medical action would be a mere placebo—that is, a fictitious remedy, which shows immediate compassion but does not heal, does not remedy or come to grips with the patient's situation.

At the beginning of the parable of the Good Samaritan, two characters, a Pharisee and a Levite, give the wounded man a wide berth and do not stop. Theoretically, they acted in accordance with the law, which prohibited a Jew from having physical contact with a corpse if he wanted to remain uncontaminated. The Samaritan, in contrast, tells us about the prophetic force of him who approaches the impure, who has "been made sin" for us (as Saint Paul says), who speaks to us of Jesus. Why does the Samaritan act this way, and why do the Pharisee and the publican act differently? How do they see the law? What is God's law? Is it always in force and applicable to every case? I am also asking with reference to a point in the Church's teaching that has always been a bone of contention: the existence of "moral absolutes".

Yes, we could say that the priest and the Levite in this parable, in making absolute one of the religion's ritual norms of purity, disregard what is central to the law: love of one's neighbor. They do not make themselves neighbors of him who needs them. Now, what is the fundamental revelation that Jesus gives us in this parable? It is above all the understanding that God's law does not consist of a series of human precepts but, rather, is a revelation of the goodness and wisdom of God. At bottom, at its deepest core, the law is the impulse to imitate God in his love for man, in his liberating and healing love. It is therefore never external to man, but is instead intrinsic to his true desire: it expresses the essential impulse for fulfillment with which God has created man; this is the impulse for love, for happiness, for divinization, which takes concrete form in precisely the relationships we have with others and with God.

When moral theology speaks of "moral absolutes" (and here, most importantly, you evoked the language of *Veritatis splendor*), the reference certainly is not to cultural or juridical precepts that, according to the teachings of Saint Thomas Aquinas, for example, have been abolished by the new law of Jesus in the New Testament. Moral absolutes are norms that affect precisely the truth of the love we bear toward God and our neighbor—that is, the truth of action that is aimed at helping man, healing him, lifting him up from his fall.

What are the moral absolutes? They are prohibitions of acts that, because of their intentional objective—that is, what the actor is trying to do—are always actions against a person. For example, euthanasia will never be an act of charity toward the person—no matter how much a subjectivist interpretation of the presumed intention behind it might be asserted as justification for this act. In this sense, the profound unity of intention and act is a necessity against all "gnostic" separation, which is to say, any desire to open a gap between intention and act. Such an assertion would run the risk of attributing to subjective intentions the ability to transform acts that are in themselves contrary to the dignity of the person. The morally absolute norms that prohibit euthanasia, for example, show that a physical act of murder against a person, even when he is in a state of suffering, can never be an act of love. Anyone who thinks otherwise deceives both himself and others. This is the importance of these norms, which serve to verify the truth of the intentions behind our bodily acts, verify the truth of our love. In his First Letter, Saint John states: "He who says 'I know him' but disobeys his commandments is a liar" (1 Jn 2:4). And the exegete Raymond Brown remarks that "moral Docetism" is thereby condemned as being a fleshless charity. Morally absolute norms are not the opposite of love; they are the path that verifies and manifests what true love is, love incarnate.

The inn in which the Good Samaritan leaves the wounded traveler is the Church. That is how Augustine interprets the parable. Is the Church not a field hospital? How is the Church, as the House of God, the place of mercy?

There has to be an abode, a house in which to lodge the wounded man and offer him a space in which to heal. This is where we must certainly see the purpose of the merciful act, the meaning of an act that is aimed at helping one's neighbor. This act does not aim simply to console; it aims to heal, to enable the man to walk again. The image of the field hospital is a very strong one and very well conceived and adapted to our current situation. We are in a state of emergency because man needs healing. It is an image that invites the Church to become a hospital and take the wounds upon herself, entering into the logic and harmony of the Good Samaritan.

We need to delve into the depths of this image. The objective of the Church is not to console but to heal and enable man to walk. And if there is an epidemic, a devastating and dangerous epidemic, a pandemic that spreads throughout the population, it is not enough to run here and there from one bed to another to deal with specific cases, one by one. It is necessary to consider the causes of the pandemic, to address those causes and remove them. Otherwise, even the most generous action against the damage would in the end be unavailing and in vain.

But the idea that there must be an abode, a house, an inn in which to heal also shows us the importance of not destroying the structure of the house in order to draw near to those who are knocking at its door. Those who are in need of healing, who are wounded, who need a field hospital, certainly need to find the load-bearing elements of the house in sound structural condition: it would not be good if they found a house in ruins. Those who need this house should find it in solid condition, capable of offering them restoration and helping them in the process of healing.

The cases that the Good Samaritan of today encounters are very complex, and they vary according to the specifics of people's lives. There are many kinds of wounds, but sometimes they are wounds of the eyes because they affect our vision of reality, and they are wounds caused by ideologies, which have overthrown certainties and good practices, leaving man in the hands of emotivism and utilitarianism. It seems as though being sensitive to specific cases is what qualifies as taking one's encounter with another seriously. Yet this attitude can lead to an adaptation of the gospel that lowers it to the level of man's capacity. The gospel's radicalism thus seems to be lost when it comes to the specifics of a particular case. A casuist would never be a martyr. How can the priest take the real-world person into account and at the same time convey that his personal, subjective circumstances do not affect the obedience that, generally and objectively, he owes to God's Word and God's law?

Yes, in a way the problem of casuistry is coming to the fore in our time, not just in a pastoral context, but also in its academic justification. I am thinking about its contemporary expressions in the English-speaking world, in the United States, where there is a certain renewed proposal of casuistry in the realm of bioethics and also in the realm of fundamental moral theology from authors like Jonsen or Toulmin or Keenan. Casuistry shares with the post-Tridentine manualist tradition an outdated vision of the law—the law seen as a legislator's arbitrary imposition, as an expression of the legislator's will. This would always involve applying that legislative will in a differentiated way that would respect the singularity of each case or the individual character of each conscience.

But if we go deeper and overcome this nominalist or voluntarist vision of the law, which is where casuistry has its origin, we see that moral law is not an expression of a legislative will but rather the wisdom that aligns realities with their goal. We could use another expression: the law expresses a truth about the good. Thus the law, including prohibitive law, makes manifest the actions that are contrary to the true good of man. And in this case, there is no room for a casuistry of exceptions or a casuistry that eliminates the reality or dramatic character of sin.

I recently read a paper by a French philosopher, Pierre Carion, assessing Pascal's debate with the casuistry of the seventeenth century. It is an impressive paper. We know that Pascal, especially in his *Provincial Letters*, confronted a certain kind of casuistry, which he identified with the Jesuits of his day, going so far as to use a very strong expression against them, because he considered casuistry "intrinsically immoral". The expression Pascal used is *Ecce patres qui tollunt peccata mundi*: "Behold the fathers who take away the sin of the world" (cf. Jn 1:29). But now, beyond the question whether or not such expressions are relevant, and beyond the exasperation and exaggeration of a debate and its more or less acrimonious tone, his position seems to me to be an important one because there are two ways to "take away sin". The phrase may be equivalent to "take away the law or render it useless" through a system of exceptions that is certainly not the treatment or custodianship that it requires. Changing divine law as if it were man's law is not a pastoral act; it is an abusive legal act. But "take away sin" can also be construed as "take upon oneself": to take upon oneself the sins of the world in order to expiate them and, through that expiation, heal man. This is the way the Lamb of God "takes away the sin of the world": he takes it away because he takes it upon himself and thus heals us, and, in healing us, he enables us to walk. The person who lies wounded by the side of the road must be taken to the field hospital, which is the Church, not only to be consoled but to be healed so that he can walk again.

There is a risk today of confusing clarity with rigidity. A clear, unambiguous teaching would be a burden, an imposition. But

clarity and rigidity are very different from each other. It is pre-
cisely clarity that enables us to see the path and move forward.
Confusion does not allow us to move and therefore results in rigid-
ity. Where does this confusion between clarity and rigidity come
from? How can the priest overcome it?

I think what is paralyzing and makes it impossible to keep
to the road is darkness. The Gospel of Saint John quotes
Jesus as saying that "we must work the works of him who
sent me, while it is day; night comes, when no one can
work. As long as I am in the world, I am the light of the
world" (Jn 9:4–5). The truth that Jesus came to bring
us, and to which the priest is called to bear witness, is
precisely a light that illuminates life. It is clarity, not the
rigidity of a formula, that generates hope and enables us to
see where we may safely take our steps, where they will
be borne up by a road that has the necessary firmness and
is oriented toward the goal of life itself. I think that illuminating conscience with this truth is the supreme form
of mercy. Is it not so that teaching the ignorant and cor-
recting their departures from the path are spiritual works
of mercy?

6. What is discernment?

You have written about the subject of conscience in various pub-
lications. Cardinal Ratzinger wrote a celebrated article on the
subject some years ago in which he warned of the danger of con-
sidering conscience to be an oracle—that is, a last and decisive
word, but one that lacks any reference beyond itself. Is this still a
danger? How can the priest shed light on a conscience that cannot
see, that may no longer be capable of intuiting the beauty of the
Christian proposal?

It is critical today to insist that conscience is not meant to be walled in within itself. A conscience enclosed within itself is no longer a conscience. When a great thinker and witness to the value of conscience like the Blessed J. H. Newman speaks of conscience, he explains that he understands conscience to be something very different from what the society of his time understood as conscience.

Conscience is not the equivalent of one's own opinion or judgment, and even less so of one's own taste and sensitivity; that would be the triumph of subjectivism. Conscience is rather the opening and submission to a truth that must be sought, honored, and obeyed in our most intimate being. So, yes, conscience becomes something that affects one's whole life, that touches it most deeply, in that center of man which the Second Vatican Council saw so clearly.

There is an important element here that Ratzinger highlights, actually, in the article to which you referred. The key issue lies in the fact that the primary relationship of conscience is not with the law, as it is set on the horizon by casuistry; it is, instead, its relationship with the truth. Just as the eye seeks out light, so conscience seeks out truth. And if it is related to the law, it is because the law is an expression of the truth of a path. The truth, which precedes and verifies conscience, is its friend. It is a truth about the good that knows how to say no and also how to put absolute limits on conscience, as an expression of the true good and of the radicalism of happiness as human fulfillment. This is the expression and form of a conscience that is truly respectful of the primacy and preeminence of truth.

"Discernment" is in vogue today. The word is rooted in the medieval tradition's discretio and in the Ignatian tradition's rules for discerning spirits. But, among monks as among Jesuits, it was

understood that the sphere of discernment did not affect the law that applied to the making of definitive choices. Today, however, our concept of discernment is so diffuse that it is also applied to what the law requires or to what is a definitive choice. But can discernment be extended that far? Would it not seem to create a contradiction in God himself, who asks for one thing from us with the law and in a specific situation asks for another? To avoid the major disasters that such an approach would engender, I would like to ask you if it would not be better to speak in terms of "verification" rather than "discernment".

"Discernment" belongs to the great Christian tradition and is an important word. But it has to be verified in its sources, as Professor Alexandra Diriart has shown in her writings. Cassian used it to throw into relief the monk's path to perfection, for which the destination had to be identified first. This reflection of the Church Fathers would be integrated by Saint Thomas into his study of prudence. Prudence always takes the destination as its point of departure and is capable of seeing, in a specific situation, which path leads us to the destination and which takes us away from it. Later on, Saint Ignatius would include this reflection on discernment in his Spiritual Exercises in order to find the will of God. The saint gives precise rules, one of which holds, notably, that one cannot apply discernment to life choices that have already been made or to clear prohibitions laid down in God's commandments. It was clear to him that discernment could not be exercised with regard to whether God's commandment was or was not an obligation for a person, or with regard to whether a life choice already made did or did not continue to be an obligation: the spirit that might suggest something contrary to a divine commandment or to a life choice that has already been made is an evil spirit that distances us from

God. Discernment in this sense must be exercised with a watchful eye so as not to fall into being deceived by a subjectivist spiritualism: it must be sure of its objectivity, the objectivity of the body and its worth. In his apostolic exhortation *Amoris laetitia*, Pope Francis refers precisely to the discernment of the body. Discernment is linked to the body: to one's own body and another's body and to the eucharistic Body—that is, our belonging to another and our sharing in the Body of Christ.

In this sense, the value of circumstances—we could say the value of the sacramental circumstances of existence—is important: God speaks to a person first and foremost through the sacramental signs of life, the circumstances of life, which in the perspective of the Eucharist assume value as an indication that God is directing us.

As far as the subject of verification is concerned, it is one that I learned and explored deeply in the light shed by the teachings and pedagogy of Don Giussani. Especially with respect to vocational verification, he saw the key as being, above all, obedience to the objective circumstances to which life leads a person. He saw verification as the free acceptance of these circumstances to establish, through the test of life and in the experience of life, whether obedience to these circumstances did in fact lead to greater fulfillment in life. He thus proposed living a hypothesis suggested by the circumstances of life to see whether the hypothesis is true, whether life is made greater, more beautiful, more just, more capable of fruitfulness. This is verification.

I understand that today, having lost the sense of divine law as lighting the way and of "forever" as the horizon, we would discover that, facing the difficulties that seem to diminish life and hem it in, people would recalculate the coordinates of their journey. Discernment without fixed coordinates can lead to a great shipwreck. Anyone who finds himself alone in this difficulty will be able to escape from it if he poses to himself the great question of the truth of his life. And it is from this truth, which includes the light of God and the promises made to him, that he can get back on course and move forward. The priest is a true companion. His role is to sustain the voyager during the storms by regenerating hope when it weakens. It is the memory of the greatness of a vocation and of how those difficulties hide a fruitfulness that is revealed if they are lived out before God.

Allow me to ask a provocative question: Would you drink a toast to the pope, or would you drink it to conscience? You have in your writings used this image of a toast that Cardinal Newman proposed in his time. Does this toast make any sense today? How does Peter, as pope, belong to the faith? What validity is there in the Protestants' criticism of Catholics when they accuse us of being "papists"?

It is a provocative pair of choices because the first gesture of a Christian conscience is that of faith. But we adhere to faith because we consider it to be the true faith, based on the veracious character of the witness, who is Christ, who offers us testimony of the Father, and based, also, on the veracious character of the Spirit, who convinces us deep down of Christ's witness.

Well, the first gesture of a Christian conscience is the choice of faith. Faith has the sacramental character of truth, in which the truth of Christ and the truth of the Spirit lie in the Church, in the tradition, and in the Magisterium. The pope is at the service of this witness of the truth of conscience. And, in its encounter with the truth, the pope is at the service of conscience. As Peter's successor, the pope is called to be, first and foremost, the guarantor of the tradition that unites us with Christ as witness, in history and in the life of the Church. The pope is therefore at the service of conscience. With an emphasis that is slightly papist, we sometimes turn this relationship around and overemphatically refer to the pope as though he were the only point of reference. Pope Benedict XVI, in his great homily at the initiation of his pontificate in the Basilica of Saint John Lateran, was specific about the meaning and limits of this reference to the pope in his service to the truth in favor of conscience.

I would therefore say that weighing the pope against conscience is fallacious. Because the Christian conscience incorporates reference to the pope; and at the same time the service that the pope renders to conscience is in reference to something bigger than himself, that lives in the Church and dwells in her. But a pope who put himself in opposition to conscience would, as J. H. Newman says, be sawing off the branch on which he sits. In this sense, I certainly share the spirit of the toast to which Cardinal Newman invites us.

7. Priests for the family

Don Livio, your history is linked with that of the Pontifical John Paul II Institute, starting shortly after its founding when you were a student there. In fact, you were the first to defend a doctoral thesis there. Later, as professor, starting more than thirty years ago, and then these last ten years as its president. It seems that, in your life, priesthood and family go together. There is no doubt that the priestly ministry has a close relationship with the family, but we priests sometimes find it hard to intuit the foundations on which to develop a true family pastorate. Why is it important for the priest to understand this centrality of the family pastorate? What should a priest do to be a true "pastor for the family"? Can the family help the priest understand his identity? In what sense are family relationships important to him? Is he not also spouse and father? Might these relationships not be the key that opens the way to linking his identity with his mission?

The mission with which I have been entrusted regarding education in matters of the family is a great gift that I have appreciated more and more in my life: I have seen more and more clearly the need for it, and its fruitfulness, in the lives of families and of the Church. I have come to realize that the mission addressed to the family made me value also the specific gift of priesthood that I have been given, and I have come to consider my priesthood as a precious and fruitful gift for families. The point of view that this mission fosters is important. As has been shown by Donati's studies, relationality is constitutive of a person. When a person is seen that way, the greatness of the relationships of which he is made is apparent: everyone is a son, daughter, spouse, brother, sister, father, mother. Because no one is without a family. Something happens in families—

Excuse me if I interrupt you, Don Livio, because the contrary would seem to be true: nothing happens in the family today, and it seems that people have to look elsewhere. Why do you say that something happens in the family?

What happens in the family is something wondrous: it generates the "we", not as an aggregation of individuals, but as an overflow of intimacy. Thanks to that "we", we can be ourselves and make our way on the path of life in all its grandeur, because we are not alone.

I understand that this vision carries with it a novelty in the view we take of man and, therefore, in looking at priestly work itself. The novelty of this view lies in its consideration of a person in terms of the web of relationships that identify him. If one takes this view, he understands that it is necessary to go beyond a sectoral pastorate, which has not been very productive in the Church, anyway. I am talking about a pastorate that is divided according to age: for example, when it is divided into a pastorate of children, youths, adults, but without seeing the relationships in which they live. Or when a pastorate is divided according to the problems to be solved, such as a pastorate among prisoners, the sick, the poor, or divided into groups and associations that are organized according to particular interests but do not consider a person in his most vital and decisive interests. If people are seen that way, and if the pastorate is divided that way, the surrounding circumstances in which a person lives and grows are lost. Whereas, when the point of departure is the relationships of which a person is constituted, then one can understand that the family is a resource. Attention to the family means giving it vitality or motivating it with a dynamism propitious to its advancement as an end in itself, rather than addressing it as just an object.

The priest is called to participate in the pastoral charity of Christ, and at the core of the priest's life is the Eucharist, which is the marital relationship between Christ and his Church. And that is how to understand the reciprocal relationship between the priest's mission to the family and the support that the family lends to the priest's vocation. We could say, in the great expression of the German theologian Matthias Scheeben, that "the family is a Church in the flesh."

The family is a Church in the flesh, in which the mystery of the Body of Christ is reflected in the human relationships that are born of man's flesh. Thus, with respect to the Eucharist, the priest understands that his celibacy is a spousal celibacy, that his body is called, like Christ's Body, to be given for the life of the Church, and also of the family Church, the little domestic Church. And, in addition, the priest learns from the domestic Church the concrete reality of this gift, its everyday character, the sacrifice that it requires, the attention to relationships. The priest learns so many things from the family!—when it is seen through the eyes of the nuptial mystery of the Church that is realized precisely through the family. And there is therefore a mutual interrelationship, a circularity, between the vocation of the family as a little domestic Church and the vocation of the priest to give himself virginally, eucharistically, to form the body of the Church in the world.

8. Is *Humanae vitae* still relevant?

Pope Paul VI's encyclical Humanae vitae *has prompted a great deal of protest against the Church ever since its publication almost fifty years ago. That July 25, 1968, was to be a fateful date in the history of the Church: the moment of great rejection, rejection of modernity, which with its science had succeeded in offering man a way to live love free of distress over the unwanted consequences of his acts. Birth control was finally possible, thanks to the pill. What reaction do you have to this encyclical of Paul VI? Is it still valid? After all these years of upheaval in the field of sex and marriage, was the encyclical a great rejection of modernity, or did it shine a great light upon it?*

Almost fifty years have gone by since the publication of this encyclical; we will celebrate those years in 2018. Yes, it is a "prophetic" text: a prophet is one who, expressing a judgment in God's name about the time in history in which he and his people live, opens a new future.

I believe that, precisely because of its character as a sign of contradiction, Pope Paul VI had the courage to say a word about human sexuality in a time of change in the cultural life of the world. He showed that the truth of love requires the intimate and indissoluble union between the unity of the flesh and the opening to procreation. Faced with a proposition that aimed to separate sex from procreation, the pope saw that, if this separation were effected, the greatness of sexuality would be lost, because sex speaks to us of a relationship and fertility. Is this not the cause of what has been called the "agony of sex" in late modernity? And is it not true that those who have wholeheartedly embraced *Humanae vitae* and practiced its teaching have shown a great vitality? I remember in that connection the witness of Kiko Argüello when he received his doctorate *honoris causa* in the Pontifical John Paul II Institute: the new catechumens took the encyclical to heart, and Kiko told us how God had bestowed on them the great blessing of families for doing so.

From another viewpoint, we could say that what *Humanae vitae* proposes is an authentic "human ecology". We often hear today about respect for nature. In that sense, contamination of the environment is considered to be among the great threats that are capable of destroying humanity. Respect for nature is highly desired, and this is precisely where a new sensibility opens up.

But rejection of the contraceptive pill is sometimes equated with that of other elements of a medical nature that manipulate the body, relegating the whole subject to the category of a kind of green environmentalism. For a Christian, "nature" is not a pagan divinity that we have to make sacred but, rather, is the "creation" that comes from God and expresses his goodness and providence.

Saint Francis of Assisi supports us in this Christian view. The term "human ecology" leads us to a much more profound reality. And it is the "ecology of relationships", of the fundamental relationships of man, that implicates the nature of the human body. There is a nature of the human body. There are some constitutive relationships, the significance of which becomes apparent when they are seen in relation to human happiness—that is, with the fullness of a love: this is where we see clearly that sex admits of fullness only when it is lived as a gift, as a reciprocal gift. Saint John Paul II's great effort was exactly that: to show the logic of the gift that structures sex and gives it meaning. In the face of a pseudo-culture that equates sex with pleasure, Saint John Paul II declares that sex embodies a reciprocal gift, an occasion for personal communion, and that this gift and this communion are what give sexual pleasure so much meaning.

The sexual gift is unique in that it demands total devotion. If something in it is held back, it is not a gift. The separation of sexuality from procreation or from the gift of love between individuals or its removal from the conjugal or family context implies a profound deformation of the nature of man, the nature of his body, the nature of his relationships. This does not mean, as is sometimes claimed, that the Church sees sex as having procreation as its only function: Paul VI's daring was precisely that of placing sex in the context of true love and showing how birth control, through periodic abstinence by adaptation to the rhythms of a woman's fertility, is not at odds with true love because it is not at odds with total devotion. Husband and wife, by changing their sexual habits and adapting themselves to the rhythm of fertility, perform a true act of love, and their conjugal unions continue to be a total gift of themselves. What is at stake, therefore, is the preservation of the reciprocal gift of sex in such a

way as to be able to fulfill man's destiny, as José Noriega
has shown.

Modernity, by centering on the individual and losing
the "we", has forgotten the meaning of generation. The
demographic collapse and scarcity of births into which
the West has fallen show that the manipulation of sex so
that it returns to being the place of satisfaction of a personal
desire for pleasure, but without any care for the intrinsic significance that it has in the human body, is a dead-
end street. It is a path that condemns an entire civilization
to sterility. I think this is the prophetic word that Pope
Paul VI had the wisdom to say. It not only communicates
a judgment but also opens up a hope. It does so, in fact,
when this judgment is embraced and heard in a way that
prompts a conversion. Perhaps we need today to recover
the culture of generation, as has been so well said by the
philosopher Francesco Botturi.

*So the light that the Church sheds on sexuality does not relate
solely to its true human meaning; it also relates to the drama
that it implies and, therefore, to the need to integrate it with the
attainment of a good and happy life. Sex life is no simple thing.
The media play on that in an ideological way, as married couples themselves know. And this makes necessary an education in
desire. In the Western cultural tradition, this education has been
called an education in virtues, among which is the virtue that
is specific to lovers, which is chastity. But to speak of chastity
today seems anachronistic—and, even more, dangerous, because
it prompts resentment. Is chastity a virtue of the past? What is
chastity? What gives it birth? Can love and desire truly mature?*

It must first be emphasized that the reality of human sexuality is crucial for life. It is crucial because it shapes our

encounter with reality, with specific persons, with the new and different, with what generates something new. In that way, it is linked with the experiences that are most fundamental to the formation of one's own identity: it is a difference that touches on intimacy and opens it to generation. Sex speaks to us of the "more" in life, of its grandeur and beauty, of the fullness that can be attained by embracing another person. One could describe this aspect of sexuality as a certain "ontological wound" because it pushes us to search for the other and gets in the way of our living just for ourselves, as Professor Mario Binasco has emphasized.

Human sexuality has sometimes been looked at askance. Although there is always a risk of the anachronistic, we can appreciate that the body, the sexual, has in a certain way been suspect at certain moments in the Christian tradition, for example in the Puritan era.

But, today, we have moved from this mistrust, which did not value sexuality as a good created in the human experience, to an ingenuous emphasis that fails to take into account the wounds that are implicit in sexuality. We need to be very realistic here, too. The experience of spiritual direction, and of counseling so many couples and families, shows how sexuality is also a problematic reality and often a wound, especially today. We could also say it this way: Precisely now, at a time when there is so much talk about sexuality, we do not have great success in living our sexuality truly or well.

It is therefore important to teach how to love, how to make the sexual impulse, which is so strong and crucial for life, and the affective experience, which connotes human relationships, an expression of love.

This is where the virtue of chastity comes in—a virtue about which there is a serious mistake, not merely of language, which confuses it with continence or virginity, but especially regarding its content. Because chastity is not the repression of an impulse or the mortification of affectivity. It is the virtue that enables impulse and affection to be an expression of the gift of oneself to another person. It is the elevation of sexuality to the personal level of love. Chastity enables sexuality to be the expression of the gift of oneself. That is where the importance of this virtue resides, as a strong capacity for action; it enables us to act, and to act with intelligence, with excellence. As Ricoeur said, virtue opens desire to its full breadth, to happiness, eschewing a focus on pleasure.

Chastity certainly requires continence, which is self-possession. But continence is not the same thing as chastity. Continence is a moment of chastity, a necessary moment of self-possession, but it is consummated in the gift of oneself.

To speak of chastity is to speak of the maturation of love, of a person's excellence in the way he fashions his acts of love. It involves the integration of desire and impulse, of affection and feeling, of fantasy and memory, of will and intelligence, and even of God's grace, in the spouses' search for "ourselves", for what truly unites them. And I mention God's grace, too, because that integration has its beginning in the gift of the Spirit. The Spirit, being Love, always generates a new beginning in man's desire. It is a new beginning that human freedom, with patience and humility, enables itself to pursue.

We priests have always had a very delicate task in helping others develop this virtue. In confession, in catechizing young people, in homilies, we have tried to show the beauty and meaning of modesty, as a reaction that protects the beauty of the sexed body. Today, the light we are called to shed may be especially necessary in the presence of a darkness that reduces sex to pleasure.

9. How is the family a part of all pastoral work?

The sacrament of the Eucharist is at the heart of priestly life and the nucleus of the marital vocation. A truly sacramental pastorate for families is obviously more than a mere "children's Mass" on Sunday. Rather, it should take as its point of departure the fact that the Eucharist expresses and realizes the unity of married couples and of family life. But how does the priest help the family live a truly sacramental life? And how does the family help the priest understand the sacramental meaning of life?

Let me answer your question by recounting an experience I had a few days ago: an encounter in Austria with a large group of more than two hundred families that included a great many children. We were more than a thousand people altogether, and you can imagine how many children there were in each family. So you see the greatness, the beauty of this group of families, with all the realities and difficulties of their lives together, to be sure.

The generosity and fruitfulness of family life in this group were very clear to me. What struck me the most were the celebrations of the Eucharist, in which the children, taught by their parents, knew how to participate with very heartfelt prayer. They participated in the celebration of the Eucharist beginning when they were very young, and the beauty of a liturgy in which all turned to Christ, the fount of love, was palpable. It was evident that the mystery that nourished the family was present, and the families bore witness to that mystery. This was a moving experience for me.

The sacrament of confession is where the priest's main role is that of physician. There the faithful open their hearts and show their wounds, asking for the healing grace of God. The priest is so often left in admiration for God's action in the hearts of the faithful.

Before giving absolution, he must make a judgment regarding the dispositions of the penitent as a recipient of healing grace. What is the nature of this judgment? The priest, perhaps more than anyone else, is a witness to the drama that people live, within themselves, to this age-old battle between God and man. But is it a battle at which, as priest, he is a mere spectator? Does he not perhaps put in his own word as the great ally of the penitent so as to make clear the light of God in the concrete circumstances of life? What are the virtues of a good confessor? How does one prepare oneself to hear confession well?

I remember very well something I was told by the professor at the University of Padua who directed my thesis in philosophy, when I told him I was going to attend seminary: "People will come to confess to you; when you see them, think first about how much faith they are showing you just by coming to you, a man like them, to tell you about their sometimes shameful frailties." This advice has helped me a great deal and stayed with me throughout my priestly ministry. It is with me still as advice that helps me maintain an equitable view of those who come to confess to me. They are testifying to their faith; they are persons the Lord sends me who have been, first and foremost, prompted and touched by grace to come to confession, to this place of mercy. I have sometimes experienced, too, that these people have been brought by Mary; I have seen that Mary, Mother of Mercy, is the beginning of so many paths to the sacrament of confession.

Let me first mention two things that will be of help to a priest in receiving a confession: an attitude of surprise and wonder at the grace that leads to confession; and second, at the same time, a respect for the truth of conversion and the moment of conversion. For a priest to act with a do-gooder's "benevolence" would be of no help to the penitent, because it means not taking him seriously. The encounter with the

Lord, if it is a true encounter, includes a real conversion. If not, we do not help people and we do not respect the mystery of grace that occurs in the sacrament.

The priest is called to bear witness to the truth of the conversion that is taking place. The judgment he pronounces is a judgment regarding the openness of the penitent to receiving absolution. There is a decisive criterion for this: how his will is disposed with regard to the bad acts he has committed. That is, whether or not he is still attached to what they involve, whether he allows God's grace to heal his desires and establish a new order in what he loves, the order desired by the Father from the beginning of creation. To detach himself from evil and return to God: here is the key to the regeneration of heart that the Lord achieves. The priest is certainly not a mere spectator: his word enters this act as the great ally of what God achieves in the penitent and of what the latter desires: to find God and be united with him.

And here is another important thing: that to confess well, it is first of all necessary for the priest to confess often himself, to live personally and frequently the path of personal conversion, to take the step by which one rejects evil and returns to God. This is what makes us understand the path of conversion taken by others, what makes us share affectionately the path of others that leads to the sacrament of confession, what makes us capable of understanding and truth.

10. What path should be offered to divorced persons in a new union?

Allow me to ask you yet another question about confession. It sometimes happens that parishioners come to confession with great feeling and desire and with the wish to be absolved of their guilt, but without wanting to change the choice that has led them to their situation—as was said some time ago: without true repentance or any intention to make a life change. Don't those who propose to receive the sacrament in this way turn it into more of a "place of acquittal" than a place of regeneration? Moreover, they find priests who justify their intentions, because they see guilt itself solely from the perspective of extenuating circumstances of will or insuperable errors of conscience, so as almost to remove all responsibility.

You understand that I am referring to the case of divorced persons in a new union who want to live a sacramental life. The Church, in accordance with a two-thousand-year-old tradition that has recently been confirmed by John Paul II and Benedict XVI, has seen that these people cannot receive the sacraments if they do not decide to live in continence, which is to say, as brother and sister. Is that not asking too much of them? Why does this practice seem too rigid today? Is it still valid? What is its meaning, and how can the Church accompany these wounded individuals?

The sacrament of confession is the place of truth and mercy. This is what people seek: something happens there; a conversion takes place. The priest is called to encourage the encounter with Christ and not to gratify the person's feelings with stratagems. He needs to consider the deeper question that people pose; it is a question about the truth of their lives, about what true happiness is, which is why they seek an encounter with Christ. This is not something in the power of the priest. The priest is a minister; he cannot manipulate the true encounter of a person with Christ. The priest is there to serve this encounter.

The person may be in an inner state in which he continues to be attached to sin, which he does not want to abandon because he is bound up in strong affections from which he cannot easily detach himself. It is a delicate moment on which the priest has to be able to shed light delicately and truthfully. The greatest difficulty may not be that we sin: God is not afraid of our sin. The difficulty is that we want to justify our sin, that we strain to call evil good. In our dialogue with the penitent, it is crucial to appeal to the truth of life and to how this truth is illuminated by Christ and by the Church. If the penitent does not see his own life through the eyes of Christ and of the Church, it is mainly due to an affective difficulty, a difficulty that derives from his desires, which disorient him and call for a new reordering. When we run aground on this difficulty, it becomes *esklerocardia* (hardness of heart) that blinds us as we carry out our acts. The priest will need to set out on a path that will facilitate the process of conversion by preparing the person to be able to open himself to receiving sacramental grace in what follows. The process of conversion should also comprise the capacity to "confess"—that is, to call his own sins by name before God and the Church. This is required not only by the discipline dictated by the Council of Trent but also by the personal truth of conversion that implies a judgment about evil reached in a way that enables him to distance himself from it.

On the other hand, there is one mistake that is sometimes made and must be avoided. It is the mistake of thinking that one of the conditions of a true confession is certainty that the penitent will not sin again. If that certainty were necessary, who would be able to confess? That is not the truth of the intention to make amends that confession requires. It is not a matter of the penitent's certainty that he will not sin again but, rather, the sincerity of his petition to the Lord that he not do so, the intention confided in prayer to the Lord to sin no more.

Regarding that intention, I recall what the English philosopher Elizabeth Anscombe wrote about the apostle

Peter. Peter certainly was sure that he did not want to betray Jesus, but when he heard Jesus say, "Before the cock crows twice, you will deny me three times", he understood two things very clearly. First, he knew that he did not want to betray Jesus, but, second, he knew that he would betray Jesus. These are two very different things. One is the inner knowledge of his own intention; the other is the knowledge, by a revelation from outside himself, that his frailty would bring about his fall. What the integrity of a confession requires is the first of these, the first kind of knowledge: authentic, unfeigned desire that entails a distancing from sin and a desire not to sin. We may thereafter be certain that we are going to fall into sin, but that certainty comes from another source.

I think this also clarifies in part the question of divorced persons in a new union. It is hard for us today to understand the tragedy of their situation, because we judge things on the basis of sentiment and concrete facts. In the case of a failed love that cannot be revived, why not offer another chance? Would it not make a happy, more peaceful life possible? The Lord answered that question when he said that a person who divorces and remarries commits adultery. No exegesis of this text admits of any doubt. Nor does the interpretation of the Church Fathers, as Henri Crouzel showed some time ago now. And adultery is not just a sin against conjugal intimacy: it is above all a sin against fidelity to God, against what he has joined together, because marriage is the place of alliance with God. Anyone living in this situation who seeks forgiveness from a priest for having broken the alliance with God by a union with another person—how can he receive that forgiveness if he does not have a change of heart?

The proper reception of sacramental absolution requires an intention not to commit again the sin that is being confessed. Confession cannot be an authorization to continue in a situation that is objectively contrary to marriage. Sex outside marriage is either adultery or fornication.

Besides, the situation of divorced persons who have entered into a new union does not affect their personal situation alone. It is in objective contradiction with the sacrament of the Eucharist. The Eucharist is the spousal sacrament of Christ with the Church. And human marriage is called to express this union sacramentally. If a union between a man and a woman becomes a sign of contradiction, in a situation that objectively contradicts the commitment that was entered into, it is impossible to associate it with the eucharistic mystery of which it should be an expression.

The formula to which you have alluded and that has been used by *Familiaris consortio*, of living "like brother and sister", has to be seen in context. *Familiaris consortio* uses it to describe the case in which, though a man and woman are living together, a return to the valid marriage is prevented because there are objective reasons that imply a duty to remain in the irregular situation of cohabitation. It might be for the sake of children born during this cohabitation or for the sake of the person with whom one is cohabiting. There thus would be an impediment to returning to the valid marriage. In this case, they may be permitted to continue to live together if there is an endeavor to abstain from sexual relations outside marriage. As long as scandal is avoided, sacramental absolution may be granted in confession and, therefore, also access to eucharistic Communion. This is an invitation to foster with the other person, the person with whom one is cohabiting, a relationship that moves toward a non-conjugal form, a non-conjugal affection. This refers not only to sexual acts but also to the shape of the entire relationship with the other person. It involves not just the renunciation of the sexual act but also the offering of a path that leads to the transformation of the way one relates to the person with whom one is cohabiting.

What I believe is key here is the experience of so many people who, out of faithfulness to the Magisterium of the Church, have borne witness to the pastoral fruitfulness of these teachings. It certainly is not a fruitfulness that is free of difficulties and falls. But it demonstrates the fruitfulness of the points Saint John Paul II made in *Familiaris consortio* (no. 84) and that continue to be valid because there is nothing in *Amoris laetitia* that indicates or points to a solution that differs from that one, a solution that is consistent not only with what has been confirmed by Pope John Paul II and Pope Benedict XVI, but also with what is evident in the Church's great tradition of fidelity to Scripture, in relation to marriage as well as to access to the Eucharist.

Yes, it is true that the apostolic exhortation Amoris laetitia *does not contain anything indicating that divorced persons in a new union who do not live in chastity may receive Communion. In any case, allow me to pursue the subject more deeply, because I see today a great concern about it among many priests. Admission to sacramental Communion for divorced persons who enter a new civil union would entail a change in a praxis that John Paul II himself saw as being founded in Holy Scripture and that Benedict XVI saw as having a doctrinal basis. I therefore understand that a change of that praxis would require an explicit affirmation of the Holy Father that would admit of no ambiguity. However, although it is not to be found in the exhortation, later statements by Pope Francis in interviews and letters seem to indicate that such a change is what he wants. How should a priest interpret these statements?*

I understand very well the difficulty for priests that you mention. Many of them have been able to accompany these faithful, sustaining them in their faith and helping them with patience to live in chastity, experiencing also the difficulty posed by someone who does not want to change his life. Yet, some people today want to propose a new accompaniment that, through discernment, obviates the subject of chastity and allows access to the sacraments for the person who lives (in Jesus' words) in adultery. On the basis of what criteria is such discernment to be exercised? No criteria are offered, just the complications of the situation, which the priest would have to judge for himself by talking with the person. In the end, the burden falls on the priest. This leaves him on his own, under great pressure from the faithful and the media.

In this context, the statements of the Holy Father that you mention, sometimes disseminated and presented in an imprecise way in the media and the press, confuse the issue still more. And they are relatively minor statements, made in press conferences or in private letters addressed to some bishops, or referring to other prelates' interpretations. But the priest wonders: Can this tradition, which is founded on Scripture and the doctrine of the Church and which the Church has always taught, be changed? And if the pope were to want to change it, should he not cite the authority he has received from Jesus Christ? If not, who assumes responsibility for it?

From the theological point of view, there is a precise hermeneutics to the magisterial statements of the Holy Father. There is a distinction between the way in which the Magisterium is exercised (with more or less authority), on the one hand, and, on the other, the object or set of truths (which must be revealed truths or truths having to do with revelation) on which it is incumbent upon the Magisterium to pronounce.

As far as the manner of exercising the Magisterium
is concerned, we must distinguish between, on the one
hand, a case in which the pope speaks by virtue of the
Petrine ministry, and therefore with the authority received
from Jesus, in fidelity to Scripture and the tradition of the
Church, and, on the other hand, the case in which he
speaks without invoking that authority, expressing his private opinion. This distinction is necessary not only out of
respect for the Petrine ministry but also out of respect for
the freedom with which the pope expresses himself. The
Holy Father is fully aware of this difference and has let it
be known on various occasions that his teaching is in his
encyclicals and exhortations. The clarification of a magisterial text is itself magisterial: it would require putting
received authority in play, with the intention of teaching
the universal Church. We can therefore say that, although
Francis has expressed his private opinion, there has not
been an authorized clarification of *Amoris laetitia*: the texts
you mention are not magisterially binding. The pope himself has emphatically called for *parrhesia*, and he does not
want us to limit ourselves to the subservient repetition of
his private opinions, just because they are his.

With respect to the subject matter on which it is incumbent upon the Magisterium to pronounce, it is the pope's
function to confirm us in the faith, in service to God's
Word, as it has been communicated to us in Scripture and
Church tradition. To avoid the Protestants' accusation of
"papism", we should bear in mind the general principle
by which, in order for any interpretation of *Amoris laetitia* to be binding, even the Holy Father's, it must remain
faithful to the words of the Gospel and the consistent tradition and teaching of the Church. In this matter we are
discussing, we are dealing with a discipline of divine law,
based on Scripture and with doctrinal roots, that has been

consistently taught by the Church. There is a lot at stake: the indissolubility of marriage, the nature of the Eucharist as a visible confession of the faith of the Church, and the visible, public character of the Church's penitential discipline. Given all of that, it must be said that a change on this point does not fall within the authority of the pope.

As I mentioned to you, and being fully aware of the confusion that many priests are experiencing in this regard, the light that is shed on us by the words of the Lord and the unbroken tradition of these twenty centuries continues to be the only path. The current context obliges us not only to be very patient with the faithful, but also to be able to illuminate them regarding the great questions that are in play: What does it mean to receive Communion? What is marriage? What is the meaning of sexuality? Only with these great questions as our point of departure will we be truly able to accompany the faithful.

What you have just said is not easy. Almost as though something about sex had been left unsaid, something that our society would have difficulty understanding. We value sex today as an expression of love. But you are saying that that is not enough. You are saying that, for the Church, sex is noble and beautiful, even sacred, only when it is part of a lifelong promise. In other words, what makes sex human is the promise made before God. Sex then allows a happy life—that is, a full life, in union with God. And therefore marriage is the primal sacrament, the origin of the alliance with God. But to ask these two people, to whom we referred in the last question, to live "like brother and sister"— would that not mean yet again that the Church is obsessed with sex? You carry the dialogue back to sex and its meaning, while our world leads it back to love and its intensity; might there not be love in these unions?

I believe we are facing a great paradox. It is really our society that is obsessed with sex, because sexuality has turned into a great web that envelops all of human experience, that is used as bait for advertising, that is present in a great part of social media programs, that is at fever pitch in the cult of the young, beautiful, and attractive body. Moreover, sexuality is offered up obsessively, even as a necessary and obligatory experience, going so far as to justify it as a compulsive experience, not linked to a personal element of love but, rather, almost as a physical need. The spread of pornography, of prostitution, of so many forms of child abuse, is an alarming symptom of a pathological experience of sexuality.

Paradoxically, while society exalts and inflames sexuality this way, it is not discussed within the Church. It seems as though a law of silence had been imposed, like a kind of guilt complex that leads her to say nothing.

And yet the Church does have a word to say here, a beautiful and precious word, a unique word: sex is a benefaction, a gift, which makes life great and beautiful and unites us with God. I would say that the Church is "an expert in love", because she has known it in Christ and in him has a singular revelation regarding what sexual love is.

Saint John Paul II's theology of the body has offered a great framework, a great vision that must be deepened and developed. The Church has something to say because she must illuminate the experience of human sexuality in the light of the truth of love. This is what interests the Church, and it is this truth of love that we urgently need today.

11. Is the truth of love useful?

Your answer enables me to address another question linked to the subject of love. Whereas Saint Paul declared that it is faith that justifies man, it is love that is considered today to be man's justification. Love suffices to justify an act that is motivated by that love. It is thus urged today that we should look benevolently and not accusingly upon couples who cohabit. It is proposed that the priest should approach couples without judging them, as though to say, "You love each other, but there is still one thing missing. Do not be afraid to go ahead and face marriage." This kind of approach has been called an "integrated pastorate". That it makes sense is understandable; but, on the other hand, even sociologically, cohabitation does have social value, since it favors marriage only after the fact and does not even require fidelity. How should this great challenge, of our young couples who cohabit without marrying, be addressed?

The important question is what love is, because it is a crucial question in everyone's life; no one can live without love, as Saint John Paul II emphatically affirmed in his first encyclical, *Redemptor hominis*. But love is at the same time a word that lends itself to error. The Church has something important to say here. She should welcome and listen to any experience of love. But it is necessary to be able to know it, illuminate it, accompany it, and heal it. In this sense, the word "integration" should be understood, not in its sociological sense, but in its more profoundly moral and ecclesiological sense. Sexuality must be integrated into the truth of love; and individuals must be integrated in accordance with the sacramental economy into the Body of Christ.

We find ourselves faced today with a new problem in the history of mankind: young people are not marrying; they are cohabiting. What is hidden behind this phenomenon? I do not mean the obvious difficulties related to work or housing, which should certainly be considered and addressed at the level of social policy; I am referring to the vision that these young people have of what makes life great and beautiful, of the adventure that is life, and of happiness, of the role of sex in all of that. There are two contending logics between cohabitation and marriage: the logic of experimentation and the logic of the gift. Devoting oneself as an experiment and devoting oneself because one believes and hopes. Life is greater than we are, and we will expand it, not by experiment, but on the basis of faith and the gift we have received. Anyone who wants to experiment and see whether he is satisfied will never be able to devote himself. "I believe in you and believe that, with you, life can be great and beautiful." That is why we marry, because we have a great hope.

Cohabitation is not simply an incomplete step toward a total gift; rather, it is a present falsification of the love that can unite these individuals: it enters upon another logic of intention. And, for that reason, the Church cannot refrain from saying to these individuals that in their choice of experiment and the provisional there is a poison that gravely threatens marriage because they have entered a logic of "experimenting" without "giving" themselves. They are fooling themselves in thinking that this can be a first step toward marriage. It is something that threatens a future decision to marry, as we can often confirm when we see that people who have cohabited for a long time and then marry quickly separate. The logic of marriage is not the same as that of cohabitation, and remedying something that is not just an imperfection but a sin requires a long and exhausting period of healing.

Staying on the subject of love, allow me to address another burning question of today: homosexuality. This is a matter of ignoring the obvious. "Who am I to judge?" Pope Francis has said repeatedly. But what can and what cannot be judged? The Church, in accordance with the words of Saint Paul, has made a very clear judgment regarding not only homosexual acts but also the inclination as such. Is this still valid? But why should we get involved in what people feel and do with sex?

The homosexual question has exploded today against the backdrop of the cultural circumstances in which we live. Homosexuality has existed throughout human history, but today it has taken on a very different socio-cultural character. It is about a demand for public, social, cultural, and legal recognition, of the same kind as that given to the union between a man and a woman and the exercise by a man and woman of their sexuality.

The sentence that Pope Francis pronounced in an interview ("Who am I to judge?") has certainly been misinterpreted. It is no doubt a legitimate and important sentence, because it indicates respect for the person, for every person, whatever his inclinations or life choices may be. No one can judge in the sense of putting himself in God's place, in the sense of expressing an evaluation of someone's situation before God. This was what Pope Francis meant by his statement, as can be deduced from its context. No one can judge the responsibility of a person—sometimes not even the person himself. It is God alone who knows.

But this does not mean that the Church cannot issue a judgment—not about the person, but about the behaviors and ideological justifications that aim to rationalize those behaviors and choices. The Church receives from the Lord, through revelation, not just a light on God, but also a light on man. There is a truth regarding human love that is expressed in creation, in the accounts of Genesis, and later in all of history up to the words of Jesus and the apostle Paul. Homosexuality is an exercise of sexuality that dispenses with the sexual difference between man and woman and is performed with persons of the same sex. This, from the point of view of the acts that are performed, expresses an intrinsically bad choice: this means that it is impossible to reconcile it with human fulfillment and communion with God. The inclination that resides in its origin, although it may not be blameworthy because it derives from involuntary psychological or relational situations, is an inclination that does not orient a person toward the good, which means that it is disordered in itself, as the Magisterium of the Church has declared with humility and respect. It is an inclination that is not in accordance with the creational order desired by God.

Sexual difference is very important: it permeates the human being, opening him to a new communion in difference and fertility. Sex is about difference and fertility—that is, about the new. And this human love that opens up to what is different is also the mark of the difference of man before God. Which is to say, the incompleteness (a certain wound, as I said earlier) that man experiences in sexuality, the need for the other, another who is different and whom man experiences in the sexed body, is the symbol of a deeper ontological difference between the creature and the Creator. It is of this mystery that Saint Paul is speaking in the first chapter of his Letter to the Romans. Saint Paul refers to the cultural dimension of the phenomenon in the history of salvation and not to persons as individuals. He traces the disorder of homosexuality back to a deeper rejection that consists of not recognizing humans as creatures and, therefore, not honoring God as God. The judgment of the Church on homosexuality is rooted in Scripture and has a rationality and evidence in human experience: sexuality lived in what is different opens to otherness and is the promise of fertility. This judgment is important because it affords a true criterion for love, avoiding a narcissistic bent that leads back to pure feeling, pure emotion that has value only in itself.

Knowing how to counsel persons with homosexual inclinations requires, first, an understanding of the drama they are living. It is the drama of a desire that cannot attain fulfillment, an aspiration to happiness that is impossible. And that is why there is a need to know how to help them integrate this desire, order it, live a true friendship with others without affective confusion.

This raises cultural and ideological questions that are so often difficult to unmask. Is there not a risk of naïveté on the part of the priest? Taking our lead from Jesus, we must distinguish between cultural dialogue, as when Jesus talks with the Pharisees, and a dialogue with a specific individual, as when he talks with the Samaritan woman. Is this a useful distinction? How can balance be maintained between speaking clearly, so as to illuminate the truth of things and render a clear judgment, and speaking intimately, to accompany individuals on the path?

This seems to me to be very important, because we need to keep very much in mind the different levels and different channels of communication in order not to create confusion. We must differentiate our answers and language, not in order to say different things, but to tell the same truth in a way that suits the various contexts of communication.

We have to have the courage, on the one hand, of a cultural judgment on certain tendencies and, above all, on ideological tendencies, such as the ideology of gender, for example. In this sense, Pope Francis spoke of a very widespread and threatening ideological colonization, because it is imposed on the primordial experience of man, of difference and fertility, with the intention of manipulating and almost eliminating these primordial experiences. But, on the other hand, beyond the cultural judgment, which has to be clear, we must know how to listen to people: when we are in the setting of a direct, interpersonal, counseling relationship, of dialogue, we need to be able to read the question and true desire that motivates people to speak. The priest, therefore, must do a great deal of listening. And he must guard against precipitately pigeonholing or labeling individuals. Every individual is unique. Every homosexual situation is different. We could say, with some exaggeration, that homosexuality does not exist but that, rather, there are many singular cases of homosexual persons' experiences that we should hear out with great attention, great respect, in order to understand the causes well, in a way that can help them in accordance with the truth of love, the liberating truth that shows the way along the path.

12. Is there a forever in the priesthood?

Let us talk about other aspects of the figure of the priest. In a pansexual culture like ours, in which so many different ways of living sexuality aspire to legitimacy, what sense does priestly celibacy make? My question is aimed at addressing precisely the radicalism of what celibacy implies—that is, a prophecy. This is precisely what our world does not accept, that there exists an ultimate truth of love. Our world can accept celibacy as one choice among many, provided that it is a case-by-case choice. But it will not accept that celibacy has a prophetic value about the meaning of sexuality as such. This is the scandal of celibacy and the risk to the Church.

What does celibacy reveal to us about human sexuality? Why is it so crucial for the Church and for society?

We are talking here, above all, about priestly celibacy as a free choice, which has its origin in a charismatic—that is, divinely conferred—gift: of those who "have made themselves eunuchs for the sake of the kingdom of heaven" (Mt 19:12), renouncing marriage.

Celibacy, like virginity, speaks to us of the ultimate meaning of sexuality: the union with God. Sexuality has a symbolic dimension: the wound of the difference between man and woman harks back to the wound of the ontological difference between the creature and the Creator. And that Creator is the only one who can fill the human heart. What the priest is conveying with his very life is that sexuality has its ultimate meaning in God, in a search for God that is carried out by means of a man's dedication to a woman and in which God is present as well, creating a new person. Celibacy speaks, then, of the greatness of sexuality, of its symbolic character, of its divine vocation. And this is very necessary for young people and married couples.

It is certainly a demanding and difficult witness today because of the pansexual context in which we live. It is a way of life that goes against the grain with respect to the banalization of sexuality. It is a gift of treasure in earthen vessels, which we must know how to care for, especially affectively.

Moreover, celibacy, like the true love that it is, speaks of a new fertility in people's lives: engendering a life of holiness. Thus, the figure of the priest appears as a father, who is rooted not in himself but in Christ. I think this is the particular value of this witness. The fatherhood to which the priest is called is a fatherhood that is not the product of his capacity, of his power. It is, rather, a gift that the priest receives to the extent that he allows Christ to act in his own acts, in his own love. It is a gift that blossoms precisely over his own poverty.

But why is priesthood a lifelong state, and around the clock? Would a part-time ministry not be better? Or a temporary one? A ministry that could be carried out for a certain period in life, as in the case of someone who is a sacristan or a "youth minister" in a parish?

The profound reason for this full-time priesthood is that it is a "vocation", not a "trade". In this vocation, the whole life and the whole person root their identity in their own mission. This idea that unites a person and his mission is an important one. The Swiss theologian von Balthasar says that a person identifies himself with his mission. It is in the mission that a person truly achieves personhood. I think this tells us something very profound about our human reality and also about our cultural situation: we truly fulfill our lives as persons, and we grow into being ourselves, to the extent that we give ourselves over to the call for which the Lord has created us, for which he loves us, to which he draws us through that charismatic sugges- tion that is the origin of every sacerdotal vocation.

On the other hand, the cultural crisis through which we are living is a crisis in which a person does not identify himself with any choice, because every choice would be open to reformulation. That is why postmodern man is always in a limbo of indecision, because he never defin- itively risks his life. It is a situation of impoverished free- dom, which never reaches the point of dedicating itself forever, and precisely for that reason it always remains unexpressed, never having in fact been risked and staked on the gift of love. At the end of the day, the priestly vocation, as a vocation forever, is also a matter of the reality of love as a gift of oneself to generate life.

The number of vocations has declined a great deal. Is it because God calls less often today? Vocation is always a divine call and a call to live in radical friendship with Jesus and participate in his mission. Do the young people of today think that this friendship can make their lives great? How does this call from Jesus to follow him and participate in his mission make life great?

I believe the problem of the lack of priests has been given a clear answer by Jesus himself in the Gospel. Jesus' invitation in response to this lack of vocations is prayer: "The harvest is plentiful, but the laborers are few; pray therefore the Lord of the harvest to send out laborers into his harvest" (Lk 10:2). And only the Father can be the source of the call to the priesthood, and only from him can come the possibility of addressing the exigencies of this disproportion between the Church's mission and the scarcity of those who respond to the mission. Pray. It seems to me that this prayer has a place in the family, in particular.

The family pastorate is also a path for the vocational question. I think the crisis in vocations is also a crisis in families. The lack of magnanimity in parents is reflected in the diffidence of their children when confronted with something truly great. I am talking about more than the number of children: about the great question of fostering in children a great and holy life. Families from which the fathers are absent when they make big choices, with omnipresent, anxious "helicopter mothers", prevent the children from understanding the Word of the Lord in what makes life great and beautiful. Because both fatherhood and motherhood produce a possessive way of life. This happens when the family, the children, the marriage itself, are just a human undertaking. In families that generously open themselves to procreation and the education of the children, a son who is a priest becomes a blessed, welcome gift. In this sense, a family pastorate is a pastorate that also bears fruit in priestly vocations.

All that said, vocations continue. They happen where, in addition to the family, a priest is able to bear witness to the greatness of the gift he has received and speaks simply about how much the friendship of Christ is capable of fulfilling one's life. When that priest lives his own constitutive relationships as a son of his family and a son of the Church, as a brother to his priestly colleagues and the faithful, as a spouse in Christ, who is the spouse of the Church, and as a father who engenders and accompanies a life of God, the youth who approaches him will be captivated by the vitality and beauty of those relationships. Because the priest renounces none of his own humanity or anything from the point of view of the truth of love. Instead, if he offers himself in a mysterious way in the sacrifice of his own sexuality, it is in order to realize his most profound meaning.

Don Livio, what is the hope that moves the heart of the priest? There has never been an easy time, and having plumbed the depths of the difficulties specific to our time, we can wonder: Why should we still "trust" in the priestly ministry?

I believe that that hope is the same as it has always been, for one thing because Christ is always the same. In the past, in the present, and in the future, he is always the same. And the fundamental structure of the human heart is always the same. The human heart today is no different from that of yesterday or from what came before. Hope is therefore founded on this verified correspondence between the gospel that Jesus gives us and the unchanging heart of man. The priesthood is an idea of Jesus, not a human invention. It is an idea of the Heart of Jesus that loves man. This is true always. It does not change. And in the life of the priesthood, we see that the good news of the gospel is always new.

What would you say to a young priest who sets out on his priestly life with joy and hope, but perhaps still with a little naïveté and trepidation? What would you say to a mature priest who, having had more experience but perhaps also having undergone a certain loss of hope, husbands the fruit he has already harvested and awaits what may still be to come?

I would tell the young priest that he should look at the essence of his priesthood, which is to communicate Christ, and root his enthusiasm in the Church and in the sacraments. That he should look at the essence so as not to fall victim to fashion, influenced by the success of his acts. And that he should build his ministry on a solid foundation, staking the enthusiasm of his life on the reality of the Church and the sacraments that he has been called to celebrate.

Regarding the seasoned priest, and I almost say this to myself, I would tell him to cultivate more and more the hope of the farmer, who sows in difficult times, too, with the certainty that God will ripen the generously sown seed in the fullness of time. "One plants and another reaps", and others will probably follow to harvest what he plants now. I would tell him to think of the good seed, of planting, in the sure and certain hope that the Lord will grow a crop that he will harvest through others.

One last question I would like to ask you on a big subject. On the Cross, Jesus placed Mary, his Mother, in John's hands, who received her as an indispensable part of his life. Jesus also asked his Mother to receive his disciple. What does Mary mean in the life of a priest? How does he receive her? How can she soften his heart and endow his eyes with a new vision? Mary the Mother of Jesus, of the unique priest—how is she that to every priest?

I am convinced that Marian devotion is not marginal in life but, instead, is at the heart of Christian life and the heart of priestly life. I mean that it is not something that is collateral to Christian life or the Church but, rather, that it is in their very heart, in their very source. The priesthood is called to rediscover every day how Mary is present, discreetly but firmly present, in the emergence of every sacrament that engenders life and transmits the Spirit to the faithful. She joins the priest who celebrates the sacrament and offers himself. She joins him in the difficult birth that one acts out in life, in history. Mary bestows humility and praise, the contemplation of the *mirabilia Dei*, of those great works that God performs in the simple life of the priest. But, above all, she gives us the hope of this Holy Saturday of history, the hope of resurrection in the future, and the certainty that it is through the tribulations of the present that our path toward rebirth in a new world lies.

IV

THE PRIEST AS PASTOR AND GUIDE IN THE CHURCH AND IN SOCIETY

A Conversation with
Archbishop Charles J. Chaput, O.F.M. Cap.,
Archbishop of Philadelphia

1. The story of a vocation

Let us start with an obvious question: Who have been the most significant priests in your life, and when did you realize you wanted to be a priest?

I have always wanted to be a priest from the time I was a young boy. Father Emil Duchêne was the pastor of my parish in Concordia, Kansas, where I was born. I saw him pray before and after Mass every day. He was a wonderful preacher, and he communicated to me the energy and joy of living the gospel.

I originally went to seminary to be a diocesan priest in Kansas. But after reading the life of Francis of Assisi, I transferred my allegiance to study with the Capuchins of Pittsburgh, Pennsylvania. In the seminary, I met some

The questions and responses in this chapter are taken from Archbishop Chaput's original interview in English.

extraordinary men, like Father Simon Conrad, the seminary's spiritual director, and Fathers Christian Fey, Ronald Lawler, and Robert McCreary, so the Capuchins very quickly became my spiritual "home". I entered the order in 1968 and was ordained a priest in 1970.

I have always had a lot of good priest-examples around me, both in religious life and throughout my vocation. I have sought them out and made a habit of learning from each one of them. When I became a bishop in 1988, I was returned to the secular priesthood, because every bishop, even if he has a religious-order background, is finally the chief priest of his diocese. I refocused my attention away from my religious vocation to the fraternity of the diocesan priesthood. And that has been a great gift, because diocesan priests are part of their people and tied intimately to their people in a way religious priests rarely can be because of their religious vocation, no matter how devoted they are to their parish ministries.

What things have you found most fruitful in your experience as a priest?

The years I served as a pastor in a Colorado parish—Holy Cross parish in Thornton—deeply formed me. It was a great experience because I had daily contact with parishioners but also did some work with the Capuchin students at the local seminary. In the parish, there were all kinds of people, those who came to church just in difficult times and those who were genuine searchers. You learn very quickly that Jesus needs you to minister to all kinds of people—the ones who are easy to like and others who are not.

When you are a parish priest, people call you "Father" even if they do not know you. They give you the kind of confidence they would never give to a father or a brother in their family. They open their souls to you. They accept your presence as the presence of Jesus Christ. And when you hear confessions, you realize that it is not really you comforting the sinner; it is Christ in you. People do not really want to know about Charles Chaput; they want to know about Jesus Christ. And it is very important that the priest should be focused on giving people Jesus Christ, not on giving himself.

The word "mercy" is worth examining. What does it mean in defining the work of a priest?

Mercy is one of the most beautiful qualities of God. Unfortunately, it is also a word we can easily misuse to avoid the hard work of moral reasoning and judgment. Mercy means nothing without a framework of clarity about moral truth.

We cannot show mercy to someone who owes us nothing, to someone who has done nothing wrong. Mercy implies a pre-existing act of *injustice* that needs to be corrected. And satisfying justice requires an understanding of truth that establishes some things as good and others as evil, some things as life-giving and others that are destructive.

The priest has to be the mercy of Jesus Christ for the world—a man who speaks the truth about good and evil, but with the voice of love.

2. Why the pastor?

The image of the priest as shepherd, following our Lord's self-description, may have unhappy connotations in today's world. On the one hand, it captures the beauty of the priest's guiding role. But, on the other hand, if the priest is the shepherd, then laypersons are the sheep. Sheep—to put it kindly—are not known for their intelligence, and this could be viewed as implying some sort of superiority of priests over laypeople.

The way Jesus uses the image, and the way Scripture actually means the image to be understood, is affectionate. Jesus is not talking about livestock. And he is not teaching a lesson about power relationships; that is a peculiarly modern illness—seeing everything in terms of power. Jesus is simply saying that the shepherd exists to guide the sheep. And a good shepherd is duty bound to feed, protect, and give his life for his sheep.

Augustine has some beautiful reflections on the role of the priest and bishop as a shepherd. But he is also very strong in reminding himself and his fellow bishops and priests that we, too, are part of the sheep, just like our people. We all share a fundamental equality in baptism, but, like members of any family, laypeople, religious, and priests have different tasks and roles. Again, it is a mistake to talk about these various vocations in the language of power. The Church is a different kind of society from the political addictions of the secular world. *Like* our people, we priests are Christians first; *for* our people, we are pastors.

So, laypeople are not just helpers of the priests and bishops?

We are equal because of our baptism, and we are all co-responsible for advancing the witness of the Church. Of course, we do that in different ways, but we are equally responsible, and not just as an expression of honeyed words but in a serious, practical way. "Clericalism" is not just a bad habit of priests. Plenty of laypeople are equally guilty of it, because they are happy to make their priests responsible for everything. If priests are responsible for everything, then they are also blamable for everything when circumstances go wrong.

Laypeople are equally accountable for all the needs of the community: preaching the gospel, building the faith, supporting the divorced, the widowed, and the elderly. We are all called to celebrate the sacraments, to care for the poor, to welcome the lonely and the stranger.

It is true that the bishop and priest have a special duty to act as Jesus Christ in keeping all the sheep connected to the gospel and the Church. But it is very important to have a profound respect for the layperson. The lay vocation is not a secondary or subordinate role in the mission of the Church.

The Lord often refers to God the Father. Can you speak a bit more about that notion of fatherhood?

Jesus is the revelation of the Father. We cannot speak about Jesus without speaking about the Father and the Holy Spirit. The Trinitarian dimension of the faith is foundational. So when we say that the priest is the icon of Jesus Christ, he is at the same time an icon of the Father. The fatherhood of God is reflected in the fatherhood of the priest.

Every priest has the same role as a father has in a family. We priests need to love the Church as our spouse and so love the members of the Church as our children. But that is because God is our Father. We are called to embody the tender loving care of God for his Church.

What people want from us or expect from us can be important, but it is much less important than our duty always to be the loving presence of Christ in their midst.

That requires a willingness on the part of priests to correct error when necessary, because that is what a good father does. Of course, if a father *only* corrects or disappoints his children, an unhappy family will be the result.

The abundant life the Lord as shepherd wants to give us priests, is it different from living an ordinary life?

Yes and no. In a sense, the priest is set apart by his ordination and re-created *in persona Christi*. But at the same time, the life of all Christians from the very beginning has been a life in the world. It is very important for a priest to understand the complexity of real life situations. That requires patience, prudence, a sense of humor, and also courage in ministering to the needs of his people. Above all, it requires love. The particular joy of priestly life comes from sharing and supporting the "ordinary" life of the people who labor in the world.

In the early Church, the missionary activity of the Church was like this. The Acts of the Apostles tells us that Paul worked side by side with a married couple, Aquila and Priscilla. They were all tentmakers. But they were also evangelists together. They worked together in the normal world, by the river, outside the synagogue. I think the future of the Church will be something similar to this.

3. What is the education of a priest?

Few institutions around the world are as demanding with the long education of their ordained leaders as the Church is. On top of that, in the Latin rite, we have the obligatory promises of celibacy and obedience. But such a demanding educational path is not always accompanied, at the end of the road, by a comparable overall maturity and judgment. Why does this happen? Are there structural weaknesses in this process that need to be addressed?

We live in a confused and confusing time. Candidates for the priesthood tend to be more fragile than they were in the past because family life is more unstable today than it once was. In the United States, there is a great deal of ambiguity about what it means to be masculine, what it means to be a man. Some candidates do not have the strong convictions they need to be real fathers to their people.

We need to do more to support and guide new priests in the first and second year after their ordination. Life in a seminary is very different—sometimes very bluntly different—from life as a newly ordained priest in a parish. New priests need ongoing counsel and help as they get accustomed to their new duties. We still have not developed a system for doing that well.

What should be the main concern of a bishop regarding the education of his seminarians? Is a talent for leadership really that vital to cultivate in new priests?

Some men are not good pastors but very good priests. Padre Pio was a wonderful priest and a legendary confessor. But I do not know what kind of pastor he would have been. Different men have different gifts.

But the diocesan priesthood really does come with the expectation that a priest will be the leader and pastor of his community. So every priest must have at least some basic leadership skills. If a priest gives up his responsibility to lead, he always has enormous problems with the faithful—*always*.

What truly happens in the ordination of a priest?

The sacrament of holy orders involves a configuration to Jesus Christ in a man's essential dimensions: in his nature and in his action. So the man who is ordained offers his humanity to Christ as a means by which Jesus can act in the world. Wherever a priest is, he is the presence of Christ.

What do you remember from the day of your ordination?

I have been ordained three times: as a deacon, priest, and bishop. To be honest, my priestly ordination was awkward. Actually, it was an awful day, because the place where my Capuchin class was ordained was not prepared for us. Also, I was very nervous, because in those days the newly ordained would preach at his own first Mass. Now we have returned to the old practice of asking somebody else to preach at a man's first Mass.

I was much more conscious of my responsibilities at my episcopal ordination, and I had already had a wonderful life as a priest, so it really was an extraordinary experience. I was not nervous at all.

The first years of ministry are a period of both special grace and difficulty for new priests. What do you think is important in these first years, when many young priests reaffirm their priesthood but others fail and lose their vocation?

The first years of priestly life are crucial. In Philadelphia, we try to match new priests with pastors who can be real mentors. But sometimes we make mistakes, because there are personality conflicts, or because someone who is a good pastor is not a good mentor. And it is vital in those moments to change the newly ordained man's assignment quickly, to recognize that we made a mistake. And we have done that.

Some candidates have dreams about the priesthood that turn out to be very different and much less comfortable in real priestly life. It is harder to be a priest than many people imagine.

4. What is the illuminating word?

In the Old Testament, the outstanding figure of a pastor is Moses: he led the people of Israel from slavery to the Promised Land. Moses is also the pastor who went from being a person "who knew not how to speak" to becoming the great public speaker we find in the book of Deuteronomy, with the longest and most beautiful speeches to be found in the Old Testament. Why is this significant? What does this tell us about the mystery of preaching?

Well, Moses would probably not be ordained today if he applied, because he was a murderer. He murdered the Egyptian who was treating the Jewish people harshly; that is why he fled into the desert. And other saints who had a history of sin would not be ordained today: Augustine had a very mixed past, and David, the great king of the Jews, committed adultery.

Good preaching proceeds from confidence; you need to believe what you say, and, at the same time, you need to forget yourself. It proceeds from confidence in God's commission to you, even though you are a sinner.

A significant detail in the life of a priest is how to manage his work-rest rhythm. In the United States, there is the tradition of having a day off, but the question is: How can the priest truly rest? Which activities are true rest, and which ones are nothing but traps that appear to bring relief but rather end up weakening and dulling the priest's mind and heart?

For me, a day off is not a day when I do not work; it is just that I do not have scheduled appointments. Because my agenda is totally scheduled, almost a year in advance, a day without appointments is like a vacation. But I cannot imagine just doing nothing. Of course, others really *like* to do nothing: and there is nothing wrong with that.

It is very important to have and spend time with friends. I always encourage priests to have priest friends, but not *just* priest friends. We also need to have lay friends; otherwise, we tend to be too clerical.

Everybody does this in a different way. There are different forms of rest. I love to read, for example. And that is a great escape for me from the ordinary pressures of life.

What kind of books?

Everything. I read quite a lot. Right now I am reading a novel, but I love reading biographies of saints, history, and of course theology. I also read the newspaper. I read at least two newspapers every day. It is important for a bishop to know what is going on, locally, nationally, and globally.

5. Does the priest engender society?

What about the care that a priest owes his own family as son and brother? How should we live pastoral charity with our own blood relatives?

When I was a young priest, my sister often reminded me that I really did not know more about raising children than she did. And it was true. When you are a priest, you sometimes give advice that is not necessary or prudent. It is very hard to preach to your own family. And maybe it is best not to try, except in an indirect way.

But having said that, I will add this: My niece died recently. She was a young woman scheduled to be married. And three months before her wedding, she was diagnosed with a terrible cancer. She died very quickly. And I had to preach to my family at her funeral as the principal celebrant. It was a hard moment for all of us because we had been preparing for a wedding and instead had a funeral.

But in the end, it was a beautiful experience because my brother and his family gave me an extraordinary example of trust in God. My family made it possible for me to act as a minister, and they offered me a wonderful Christian witness of faith at the same time.

Now, we also need to understand that sometimes God calls us to make tough decisions in opposition to our families, in order to be faithful to the gospel. The priority for all of us is Jesus Christ. And that priority is above family, above spouse, above mother and father.

Our society tends to compartmentalize people's lives in separate spaces: work, family, entertainment, friends, and so on. How can the priest give unity to all these spheres in the life of his people? How can the priest help people not to get lost in these different spaces?

Americans are individualistic by nature, and the result is a culture of separation and self-absorption. There is a much better sense of community in the immigrants that come to the United States from Latin America. They have a healthier sense of mutual dependence. For them, your personal identity is not simply defined by your personal success. And your greatest achievement is not how much money you have, but how many good friends you have.

To be a Christian means to have a sense of people, of concrete persons with whom you share your faith. And so priests need to foster and encourage smaller, more intimate communities—beginning with families—in which this gathering and sharing can take place. If a priest can promote real communities and intense Christian living, that is the best way to overcome the risk of social fragmentation.

An important aspect of a parish priest's work is his interaction with all sorts of civic institutions, schools, health centers, and businesses. How best can he deal with the people in charge of all these institutions? Taking a broader perspective, why is the Church interested in having a presence in society's institutions?

Even if it is difficult, it is important for Christians to be active in the public square, because if *we* do not get involved, other people will—people with different and antagonistic views about the gospel. We need at least to try to make the world a better place. Being a Christian is not just about my private relationship with God. Faith is never private. It is always personal but never private. And because it is personal, it has interpersonal, community dimensions. I am my brother's keeper. We have a responsibility for other people around us, and not just for ourselves.

In the past, the Church was usually seen as a partner in building a good public community, especially in areas like health care, education, and social welfare. But the more secular the United States becomes, and the more people ignore the beliefs and values of the Church, the less we are welcome in the discussion of public issues. But that should not keep us from making our voices heard in the world.

Sometimes the only counsel we hear from our pastors and bishops is to "vote according to our conscience". But, is this useful advice? The problem seems to be that an individual conscience is not an oracle and that what people need are clear criteria by which to form their consciences.

All moral issues have a natural hierarchy. For example: It is bad to lie to your friends. It is worse to steal from your employer. It is worst to murder your neighbor. All these actions are evil, but common sense and a healthy conscience dictate that some things are more evil than others.

In like manner, helping the poor, feeding the hungry, providing shelter for the homeless—all these issues are vitally important. But the intentional killing of innocent life through euthanasia, deliberately targeting civilians in war, genocide, and abortion directly attack the right to life itself. The right to life is not just another important issue; it undergirds all other rights. In other words, it is *foundational* and takes priority over all other issues. This is why no program of social progress can ever succeed if it allows the killing of unborn human life.

The American bishops said exactly this in their 1998 pastoral letter *Living the Gospel of Life*. It is the best practical guide to political conscience-formation the U.S. bishops have produced so far.

6. Does celibacy make the priest great?

What about celibacy? Some experts in sociology have labeled our society "pan-sexual": all is related to sex. Is it possible for a priest to live celibacy nowadays? Is the Church asking the priest for something that is not human?

The more basic question is whether it is possible for *anyone* to live the Christian teaching on sexuality today. Can married couples be faithful to each other for life? Can engaged couples love each other without having sexual relations until matrimony? The debates over celibacy for priests are only one small aspect of the modern assault on any form of sexual restraint.

In any age but our own, the idea that a fruitful life cannot be lived without sexual intimacy would be regarded as insane.

Celibacy is not just a Christian or Western tradition, and the experience of celibacy in the Church goes back to Jesus (especially in Matthew 19:12) and to the teachings of Paul. It is not something we can change just because the modern world finds it strange and inconvenient. The Christian view of sexuality is not something new. The time of Saint Paul was not so different. The real disaster is that our sexual confusion has undermined family life, which has huge and very negative consequences in the lives of children and the life of our whole society.

Pope Francis has encouraged us to help the poor, but he has warned that the Church is not an NGO. What is the real meaning of social work for a priest?

We will all be judged on how we feed the hungry and help the poor. That is true for the priest, and it is true also for his community. Helping the poor is a serious obligation for every Christian.

But, in a sense, social work is the easiest part of a priest's ministry. Even people who do not want to change their lives feel better if they give money to the poor. It is much more difficult over time to be generous, forgiving, and faithful to one's family and friends, to anchor our joys and sufferings in the love of God, and to sacrifice our time and energy for others than to give money to the poor.

We cannot reduce Christianity to caring for the material needs of the poor. If we do that, we ignore the deeper demands of our faith. The Christian motive for helping the poor is very different from humanitarian do-goodism. It has a *religious* purpose linked to the healing of souls and the sanctification of the world by bringing the presence of God into the lives of people who suffer.

Is there a special way for a priest to pray? And a special need to do so?

We cannot survive as believers if we do not pray. That is just as true for priests as it is for laypersons. If we do not pray, what faith do we really have? Prayer is a conscious relationship with God. No one can be a believer without praying.

The unique way for a priest to pray is to lead the sacramental life of the Church. And the special temptation of the priest is to be a religious "professional" or a gifted liturgical showman. But that is a form of acting; it is not really prayer.

When we genuinely offer ourselves to the Father as priests with Christ, that is prayer. The duty to pray the Divine Office every day is a gift that we have from the Church. I have been doing this for fifty-seven years now as a religious and as a priest. And I find something new in the words all the time.

Sometimes a priest needs to live alone because of his assignment, but what are the roles of brotherhood and friendship with other priests? How can a community with other priests help him in his vocation?

The natural community of a priest is his parish, the people he is called to serve. Of course, it is also important for a priest to have good relations with other priests, because we have a shared experience that others do not have. And with other priests we can speak more directly about problems, experiences, life in the ministry.

I encourage priests to form support groups, and I have belonged to one myself for many years. We meet frequently and examine our lives candidly; we pray together; we have confession. And I think this is really essential, because we priests need the encouragement of people who know what our life is like from experience. They can give us what other people do not.

Spiritual direction is vital for a priest. But it is also important just to have fun together with other priests, to go to dinner together and not be isolated.

You come from an experience of religious life as a Capuchin. How has religious life enriched your priesthood and your mission as a bishop and as a diocesan bishop?

It was strange for me when I became a bishop. For the first time in my life, I was praying the Office alone. I had always prayed it in common. In a sense, it is harder to pray by yourself than when you are with others. I have already mentioned the importance of priestly community, of friendship, of belonging to a creative minority. Religious life brings all that to the priesthood in a special way.

But, on the other hand, as a diocesan bishop I have also now experienced what it means to be a pastor, what the pastoral leadership and guidance of a concrete community actually entail.

The ministry of preaching is not always easy. Sometimes the priest falls into a kind of repetitive moralism; other times, his word becomes too abstract, with no real effect in touching the lives and the hearts of his people. How should the priest preach?

I love to prepare homilies. I read Scripture commentaries and homilies of the Church Fathers on the particular passages of the day, and I also use other resources. And I get ready for the Sunday homily well in advance. Every day, in the first two hours of the day, I have some time on my own to study, to pray, and to read. And part of this time is the preparation of the Sunday homily. I do not prepare as well for the ordinary daily Mass. I just cannot. But it is essential for me, for my mind and heart, to be able to say what I want to say.

Priests have a great responsibility before God to preach well. Obviously, some men have more natural talent than others. But people in the pews always know who has prepared well and who has not. One of our sins, a common sin of Catholic priests, is that we do not take preaching seriously enough. Actors or professional orators get fired if they do not speak well. We never get fired.

And it is very important to preach what the Church and Jesus have said, not our own opinions. Saint Francis urged his men to preach the gospel without gloss. And for me that means "without excuses", without explaining away Scripture's difficult commands. Our personal sins must not stop us from preaching. We need to preach the truth even if we do not always follow it ourselves. Of course, we should be led by the shame of our sins actually to live what we preach. But our sins or our fears or our eagerness to please our people should never prevent us from speaking the truth.

7. What can we hope for from a priest?

Is the priesthood such a high ideal that it can become unrealistic for human beings? Should we reduce our expectations about what a priest can give?

Jesus Christ is the measure of the priest, because we are other Christs in the Church. And that is an impossible ideal if we do not believe it to be true. But Christians believe that priests are chosen by Christ and that he uses those of us who are priests as his voice in the world. And our work as priests is to make ourselves free to be his voice. Free from our self-preoccupation, free from our sins, free from our own prejudices, so Jesus can use us as he wants, as his voice.

This is not merely an ideal. This is something real: We are "other Christs" in the world. The mystery is *why* Jesus would want to use ordinary people as his friends and collaborators in reaching the world, men without particular skills, men who are sinners. In the Gospels, we see that none of the disciples of Jesus really understood him. And yet he chose them to share his mission. Peter was not more talented than the rest of us. But Jesus chose him very quickly. Paul was a persecutor of the Church. Jesus also chose him.

Our Catholic vision of ministry is very different from what Protestants typically think. They tend to see ministry as leadership; we see it as *configuration*. Leadership depends on natural talents, and of course natural talents are a great gift. But Catholics believe that in the sacrament of holy orders, by an extraordinary grace, a literal configuration to Christ takes place that makes us icons of Jesus Christ.

A priest should have "the good odor of Christ", as Paul said. What does this mean? But the pope also asks the priest to be close to the sheep and to "smell like sheep"—how can we reconcile these two notions?

They are easy to reconcile. You can smell metaphorically like both.

Most people do not understand what Pope Francis meant when he used his phrase about smelling like sheep. He was stressing that a priest needs to ensure that his life stays in contact with the reality of his people. But of course, first of all, we need to keep our priestly lives in contact with the Word of Jesus Christ. That is the beauty of the holy oil with which we are signed on the day of our ordination. It represents our configuration with Christ as priests. It is also used in baptism and in confirmation where we are configured to Christ as believers. This oil has a beautiful fragrance to remind us that we need to be the fragrance of Christ in the world. The important thing is not to smell like sin.

Are the sacraments just "another part" of the life of a pastor? Are they just isolated appointments in his schedule? What does it mean for a pastor to live a "sacramental existence"? Why is this so important in our day?

For a priest, the sacraments are everything. They are our prime responsibility. On the day of our ordination, we were configured to Christ for the Church. But that is only fully realized in the Eucharist and in the celebration of the sacraments. The priest acts in the name of Jesus Christ, who is present in the Church through the priest's sacramental actions.

We can never minimize the centrality of the Eucharist in the life of a priest. When a priest celebrates the Eucharist, he summarizes and offers to God everything in the life of the Church, his preaching, his personal life, his community. All is offered up with Christ to the Father. The cross is the center of the Eucharist and the center of a Christian life. It is the symbol of self-giving, which is what the Eucharist is all about.

All the other sacraments find their meaning in the celebration of the Eucharist. If a man does not want to celebrate the sacraments or if he experiences them as a burden, he should not be a priest. He can be a lay preacher, a lay adviser, a lay comforter of the sick, but he cannot be a priest.

Pope Benedict XVI spoke some years ago about the importance of "creative minorities" prepared to live and transmit Christian hope in modern, unbelieving societies. But how we can do this? How can we work to generate these "creative minorities"?

Small communities help people share their faith on a more intimate level. They are urgently needed in today's secularized cultures. Modern life has a veneer of confidence and comfort but also a very strong undercurrent of despair.

As Benedict cautioned, these small Christian communities cannot be ghettos; they need to be outwardly focused, welcoming, and missionary. We cannot be Christians alone. We need to be Christians together. The parish structure is often too big and formal to foster close faith relationships. So we also need these smaller creative communities. Priests should warmly encourage them, while also helping them stay rooted in, and fruitful for, the larger parish community.

What would you recommend to a young priest who might be starting his ministry in a parish, full of great expectations but with very little experience in life? What would you recommend to a mature priest, with lots of experience and faith, but who may have lost some of his hope and passion, disheartened by the frustrations of the expectations he happily had when he was younger?

My counsel to each of them would be the same: Take care of one another. The older priest needs to learn from the younger man what the expectations of young people are for the Church, but he also needs to share the wisdom of his experience. An essential part of being a father is being a mentor.

We priests do not get married, we do not have children, but we can be pastors and pass on our experience of Jesus Christ to the next generation. And we also can learn from them. The younger generation always brings an entirely new perception of things. They can help us be much better priests. Just as we mentor young laypeople, we have to mentor young priests. And young priests need to see that they should learn from older priests, who have experience. They should respect the older priests, but they should also learn from them and not be afraid of them.

The unity of the priesthood is accomplished by the older being engaged with the young and the young wanting to be engaged with the old. We need to encourage this. It will not happen naturally. Naturally, we go with the people of our same age, the people with whom we are comfortable. We need to go beyond that.

What I would say to each separately would be this. To the older ones: "Brothers, understand that you are getting old, and the Church is different today from what she was in the past. We cannot be committed to old forms of priestly life that are no longer working. Whether they work or not should be the task of the new generation to judge. Try to be pastors who are grateful to be remembered for your work."

And for the young I would say, because the younger are always in danger of being discouraged: "The Resurrection of Jesus and his Ascension to the Father are not legends or beautiful stories. *They are real.* They are historical events, and we need to trust the gospel with our lives. God sent his Holy Spirit over all his creation and to dwell among us. That is true. That is factual. And that gives us hope in the midst of discouragement. Like John at the Cross, take Mary into your heart as your mother, and she will accompany you always."